Powertul People Are Inspired by Powerful Athletes

CREATING A CULTURE OF CHARACTER

Power Series

PRODUCING A PERSONALITY OF POWER

www.bepowerful.net

What People Are Saying

As someone who has made a living and a career out of interviewing athletes in all types of situations, I find *Powerful People Are Inspired by Powerful Athletes* to be very inspirational and important for anyone to read. Athletes are role models whether they choose to be or not, and we have seen their influence over entire communities, countries, and sometimes even generations. This book teaches us the principles that many of these athletes share and how we can learn from their experiences.

~ Chris Myers—Fox Sports

There are no limits to what you can achieve! This book illustrates a champion's passion, attitude, and inner thoughts that can also be applied to any aspect of life by anyone. Very inspirational, life changing book!

~ Janice Gibson—LPGA Tour Player

As the Good Book says, "Faith without deeds is dead." This collection of inspirational thoughts addresses both the ideas of success and how to put them into practice. Great athletes are born, but they do not achieve greatness without a firm commitment to excellence, and the hard, daily work that gets them to that special level. Each one of us can strive to be our best, and these words can be a spiritual and practical guide to running the race of life, which is not a sprint, but a marathon.

~ Bob Carpenter—Sportscaster, Washington Nationals,
ESPN Regional TV, and University of Oklahoma

Jeff Brucculeri and his book *Powerful People Are Inspired by Powerful Athletes* points out the importance of influence and power that is created by encouraging words and quotes. As I have served with the Fellowship of Christian Athletes for almost two decades now, I have found that the most important key to this ministry work is the simple influence that coaches and athletes have on fans, teammates, opponents, and peers. Most often through their words and ours too, can we pass on encouragement and empower others to greatness through what we share and how we say it. This book will help all those willing to engage and learn from what the power of just a few words can do for themselves as well as others around them.

~ Chris Kaiser—Northeast Oklahoma FCA Area Director

In a quarter-century of reporting on sports, I have often heard high school and college coaches say they are preparing their players for life outside of athletics. Many of the strategies that make teams and players successful can apply to all of us in our everyday lives. All winning teams and athletes need to take a time-out occasionally to examine where they've been and where they are going. They need a game plan. *Powerful People Are Inspired by Powerful Athletes* can help all of us game plan and analyze our lives for more powerful living, while also giving us an inspiring quote to carry with us from many sports figures we've admired. For me, it's a good way to either start or end the day.

~ Barry Lewis—Sports Writer, *Tulsa World*

Start to Finish

Starting can be easy, but it's …
The last mile of the marathon
The last yard to the end zone
The last buoy in the regatta
The last turn on the speedway
The last inch to the cup
The last foot in the dash
The last second in the game
The last pitch to the batter
The last hill in the journey
The last stand before the bell
The last ledge to the summit
The last stroke in the match
… That counts; because, if
You don't finish, it doesn't
Really matter who is first or last.

~ Vanposetski

About the Book Cover

The *'Power~Series'* book covers are designed by the authors using the human hand. The hand symbolizes:

Love	—	Holding hands
Cooperation	—	Showing hands
Support	—	Helping hands
Work	—	Busy hands
Sustenance	—	Cupped hands
Celebration	—	High-five hands
Worry	—	Wring hands
Thanksgiving	—	Praying hands
Applause	—	Clapping hands
Direction	—	Pointing hands
Security	—	Clutched hands
Communications	—	Signing hands
Supplication	—	Folded hands
Morality	—	Clean hands
Power	—	Fisted hands
Peace	—	Shaking hands
Giving and Receiving	—	Open Hands

The game of sports can not only be symbolized by many different and variously styled hands, but by the entire body. Athletics come in various forms and almost all physical activity can be considered a sport of some sort. However, the most common thought that comes to the authors' mind's eye, when we think of athletics as sports, is depicted on our cover. Regardless of your particular game, event, or match, there is so much to be learned and gained from those involved in every sport. This book presents inspiring words that have come from coaches, athletes, media members, and philosophers in general, that pertain to athletics. Their wisdom applies to all of our lives regardless of what sport we enjoy or even if we are not athletic at all.

CREATING A CULTURE OF CHARACTER

Power Series

www.bepowerful.net

PRODUCING A PERSONALITY OF POWER

The Power of ONE

The *'Power~Series'* books are all about changing the world—a globe rife with secularism, moral decline, egalitarianism, and human denigration. It is the purpose of the books to evaluate the human soul—its mind, body, and spirit. Through the books and the words of the authors we wish to create a culture of character and produce a personality of power. The writers intend to make this big change for the better, *one* day, *one* person at a time. They call it the Power of ONE.

Key Terms and Phrases

Culture of Character: In the *'Power~Series'* books, the term refers to a shared way of life in a particular social group or an individual's circle of influence that personifies virtuous values, sound ethical practices, and moral excellence. It is a wholesomeness that is manifested in a sound mind, a healthy body, and a stellar spirit. It is shown in a person's certitude and consciousness. It is a way of life embodied in a self-purpose of goodness.

Personality of Power: In the *'Power~Series'* books, the phrase describes the individual attributes (behavioral, temperamental, emotional, and mental) that are unique to power performers and powerful people. For a more complete description of a powerful person, please refer to page one in this book. To learn more about the traits and qualities of power-driven people, please read of them in the *'Power~Series'* books: their thoughts, weltanschauung, self-purpose, and living life actions.

The 'Power~Series' Books

The 'Power~Series' books are all about acquiring, building, and maintaining a culture of character and a personality of power. They mean what they say and say what they mean. They are powerful and contain the dynamism to make a person like you a more power-driven individual. The books are about the readers learning how to effectively acquire and utilize productive power in all facets of their lives, personal and professional, at home, work, and play. The books are not concerned with dominion, authority, and control. These books are about health, wealth, harmony, happiness, and wisdom. The 'Power~Series' books will provide you with the principles and practices that produce a lifestyle full of wellness, insight, and success.

Many elements make a powerful person. Such essentials as teamwork, relationships, leadership, networking, teaching, meekness, listening, learning, spirituality, character, and health make a short and incomplete list. The material and information in the 'Power~Series' express what it takes to be powerful in living life. The aforementioned areas are part and parcel of the essential elements contributing to the makeup of a culture of character and a personality of power. The syllabus can go on ad infinitum. Currently, 'Power~Series' book titles include:

Powerful People Have a Powerful Big "i"
Powerful People Have Powerful Character
Powerful People Have Powerful CHEE
Powerful People Overcome Powerful Failures
Powerful People Play Powerful Golf
Powerful People Are Powerful IT Professionals
Powerful People Are Powerful Leaders
Powerful People Lead Healthy Lifestyles

Powerful People Have Powerful Meekness
Powerful People Are Powerful Networkers
Powerful People Are Powerful Performers
Powerful People Are Powerful in Prayer
Powerful People Have Powerful Relationships
Powerful People Are Powerful Teachers

More Titles Will be Released Each and Every Year

Powerful People Have Powerful Attitudes
Powerful People Age Powerfully
Powerful People Have Powerful Children
Powerful People Are Powerful Dreamers
Powerful People Are Powerful Givers
Powerful People Are Powerful Healers
Powerful People Are Powerful Learners
Powerful People Are Powerful Listeners
Powerful People Have Powerful Marriages
Powerful People Have Powerful Money
Powerful People Think Outside the Box
Powerful People Have Powerful Parents
Powerful People Have Powerful Personalities
Powerful People Are Powerful Preachers
Powerful People Are Powerful Readers
Powerful People Are Powerful Risk Managers
Powerful People Are Powerful Speakers
Powerful People Are Powerful Soul Winners
Powerful People Were Powerful Teens
Powerful People Are Powerful Travelers

To learn more about the *'Power~Series'* as well as to order additional *'Power~Series'* books, please visit www.bepowerful.net. Publishing the *'Power~Series'* books is the exclusive production of Peter Biadasz and Richard Possett. You can learn more about the producers in the **About the Authors** section of the book you are holding in your hands. If you have an interest in coauthoring a *'Power~Series'* book with Peter and Richard, please e-mail them the subject matter that you have expertise in and are passionate about together with a short personal résumé at www.bepowerful.net. Thank you!

Powerful People Are Inspired by Powerful Athletes

Your Daily Guide to Powerful Life Lessons

Peter Biadasz, Richard Possett
and
Jeffrey Brucculeri

Foreword by John Anderson, ESPN

iUniverse, Inc.
New York   Bloomington   Shanghai

Powerful People Are Inspired by Powerful Athletes
Your Daily Guide to Powerful Life Lessons

iUniverse books may be ordered through booksellers or by contacting:

iUniverse
1663 Liberty Drive
Bloomington, IN 47403
www.iuniverse.com
1-800-Authors (1-800-288-4677)

Because of the dynamic nature of the Internet, any Web addresses or links contained in this book may have changed since publication and may no longer be valid.

The views expressed in this work are solely those of the author and do not necessarily reflect the views of the publisher, and the publisher hereby disclaims any responsibility for them.

ISBN: 978-0-595-51270-6 (pbk)
ISBN: 978-0-595-61830-9 (ebk)

Printed in the United States of America

Tributes

This book is dedicated not only to the many great role models with whom I have been blessed but to those who through their daily, positive, and consistent influence, serve as role models for people of all ages.

~ Peter Biadasz

I have had the wonderful experience in life to know Steve Largent, a member of the Pro Football Hall of Fame and a great person. We sat next to each other watching our sons play baseball as teammates. I worked with him when he was a Congressman. In the 'Power~Series' we speak to a culture of character and a personality of power. All that Steve Largent is, as an athlete, a father, a husband, and a person, truly exemplifies these essential elements for being a powerful person. For all these reasons, I dedicate this book to him.

~ Richard Possett

This book is dedicated to all the athletes I've come in contact with throughout my life, and there have been many. As a fan, as an employee of several minor league sports teams, as a sports broadcaster, as a coach, and as a sports official, I have had the privilege of meeting, interviewing, mentoring, and forming relationships with literally thousands of athletes. Many of these athletes have been truly great people to know, while others left a lot to be desired in the role model category. I've learned from them all.

~ Jeffrey Brucculeri

ath • lete

NOUN

This is a sportsperson, an individual, a competitor, who is trained or skilled to participate in athletic events, exercises, sports, or games requiring physical strength, agility, and stamina. Athletes don't just show up for events, they plan and compete, engage with passion, have detailed schedules and lofty goals, eat right, arduously train, maintain positive mindsets, persistently persevere, work very hard, are courageous, compassionate, and people of noble character.

~ Peter Biadasz, Richard Possett, and Jeffrey Brucculeri

Why Read This Book?

Powerful People Are Inspired by Powerful Athletes—*Your Daily Guide to Powerful Life Lessons* is the book for you if you want to be powerfully successful in your life. The debate has raged for many decades whether athletes should be held as role models, and the fact is, since the beginning of time, athletes have been held in high esteem. Right or wrong, that's just the way it's been since the first race was run in Ancient Greece and someone was declared a winner. The winner has always been celebrated by the adoring public. However, over the many centuries of athletic competition we have learned that some of those athletes whom we have put on a pedestal may some day disappoint us.

Some athletes wield a lot of power based only on the fact that they've signed huge contracts and their teams are willing to do anything to keep them happy and playing well. Other athletes exhibit their power in a more positive way. The athletes we refer to as "powerful" are those who have positive attitudes about life, and they understand their role in the entertainment field in which they get paid very well to perform. However, some powerful athletes aren't even professionals at all, and they play or coach only for the joy of the sport and for the satisfaction they get from helping others. Athletes who give back to their communities with their time and money are powerful. Athletes who visit sick children in hospitals because they want to and not out of obligation are powerful. Athletes with the desire to learn and continue to improve their skills all along the way are powerful. Athletes with the discipline to practice, practice, practice, and never give up even after they've reached the pinnacle of their profession are powerful.

These same attitudes of giving and continually wanting to grow and learn more will help you to be more powerfully successful in all aspects of your life, whether you are an athlete or not. The more you cultivate these kinds of attitudes, the more you will build a mental model that will inspire you to make the kind of daily decisions that spark motivation in a way that appears to be almost magical. Your success is about growing, learning, striving to reach the top, and giving to others. It's about immediate results and long term benefits. It's about leaving a legacy. It's about being powerful.

Do you want to be a more powerful person—powerful at home, at work and at play? Of course, your answer is a powerful YES! But, genuine power is not mere physical strength. Real power is the ability to get along with your family members and coworkers. It's the capacity to motivate others, create relationships, and influence people. Real power is having a vision and communicating that vision to others, empowering others to be their best. Really powerful people model powerful behaviors and inspire others to action, sometimes without even speaking a word.

Right now you are reading a one-of-a-kind book. There is nothing else like it on the bookshelf. The text is unique because of its multidimensional nature. It is a practical, inspirational, and educational workbook. By design, this book is simple to read, and the assignments are easy to complete. It's the way to utilize your full potential. This book is a once-a-day excursion into becoming a proactive learner and thus, a more powerful person.

Read this book, examine the material, and put it to work in your own life. By the time you are finished, you should be a more powerful person with new-found strengths in your personal and professional relationships. As you progress through this manuscript, you will discover both your good lifestyle patterns and your dysfunctional behaviors. You will grow more powerful each day by building on your strengths and eliminating your weaknesses.

Through the daily lessons, you learn an inspirational quotation. By completing the daily lessons, you become a more knowledgeable and effective person. When you research the authors, you become a better-rounded individual. By being a more conversant, learned, and interesting person, you become more powerful to all those around you and your "circle of influence."

A bonus in the book is that you can add depth to your activities as you go through the material a second time—by completing the lessons in six months and adding to your work in the following six months. This process gives you an honest chance to critique your investment and make the appropriate adjustments. It enhances and reinforces your efforts to add power to your life. By learning the daily lessons and applying one skill each day into your personal and professional world, you will become a powerful person reaping wonderful rewards in the workplace and in all of your relationships. Work on it and make it work! Become a powerful person.

Contents

What People Are Saying iii

About the Book Cover vi

Key Terms and Phrases vii

The 'Power~Series' Books viii

Tributes xiii

Athlete Defined xv

Why Read This Book? xvii

Foreword xxi

Preface xxiii

Acknowledgments xxv

The Discourse xxvii

Introduction 1

- What (or Who) Is a Powerful Athlete? 1
- What (or Who) Is a Powerful Person? 1
- How to Use This Book 2
- Six Months Review 2
- Sample Illustration 3
- About the Quote Sources 5

Daily Quotes and Exercises for Powerful Life Lessons 7

- January 1–July 2 7
- February 1–August 2 38
- March 1–August 31 67
- April 1–October 1 98
- May 1–October 31 128
- June 1–December 1 159
- July 1–December 31 189

The Finale 191

Congratulations! 193

The Chuncated Learning System 195

Conclusion 197

About the Authors 199

A Note from the Authors 203

Index of Individuals Quoted 205

Index of Topics Quoted 211

Foreword

I learned very early into a very mediocre college Track and Field career at the University of Missouri the very essence of athletic competition: sometimes the other guy is just better. It's just that plain and simple. There's Tiger Woods and the rest of us hopelessly striving to match Tiger Woods.

The lesson then was one of self awareness. It was an epiphany that success for each of us is based on maximizing the potential of our natural gifts and managing the dignity of our effort. The realization that the best we can be is completely up to us and doesn't need a trophy for validation or a newspaper headline or an ESPN SportsCenter highlight.

We can't have Tiger's game but we can have his winning attitude. We can have his discipline and dedication to hard work. We can have his determination to succeed. All those things are independent of ability and things we directly control.

That's powerful thinking! That's empowering for reaching goals.

Thanks to Jeff and the other authors of this book, the best you is now in your hands in the form of an easy to follow and inspirational daily guide. It's a powerful tool for turning "I can't" or "I won't" into "I might," into "I'll try," into "I can," and finally into "I will."

The critical difference between "I can" and "I will" is commitment and action.

Make that commitment today. Take that action today. And let this book help you find the way.

~ John Anderson
ESPN SportsCenter

Preface

We are all sports fans and, believe it or not, we can truly learn from some of the interesting things that are said by athletes, coaches, broadcasters, and others associated with the games. We can also learn from some rather interesting quotations about athletics and the thrill of competition. Many people are extremely passionate about sports and their favorite teams; that's why we're called *fanatics*. However, if we were to apply that same zeal and passion to our everyday lives, to our careers, and to our relationships with our families, then we would truly become powerful in all aspects of our lives. Many athletes become great at their particular sport for a reason beyond just sheer talent. The reason amateur athletes become great professional athletes is that they have a strong passion to succeed and to never give up. They have the desire, determination, dedication, and discipline it takes to reach the top of their profession. That's how we should approach our life—with that same desire, determination, dedication, and discipline.

The principles in this book have been gleaned from long and productive business careers and a passion for athletics. We walk the walk. We practice what we preach. We are confident that the quotations in this book will inspire you to do the same. They should take you beyond mediocrity on the field of play, on the court, on the job, and at home. Completing the daily lessons will make you a more dynamic person. Please read and fill in the blanks for your life, and enjoy. We pray that you have a great day and a better tomorrow as you grow your way to awesome effective living.

~ Peter Biadasz, Richard Possett and Jeffrey Brucculeri

(Before proceeding, turn to **About the Authors** near the end of this book to read more about the authors. Their life histories, work experiences, and expertise may give you a better frame of reference, insight, and perspective regarding the contents of this book.)

Acknowledgments

Thank you to my family, my friends, and business associates; you add so much to my personal and professional life. Even though I may not always show it, know that my appreciation runs very deep. (Yes, I have said this before but one can never say it enough.)

~ Peter Biadasz

I played baseball, tennis, golf, racquetball, basketball, hockey, rugby, and ran many races. I was never in the elite group, but I always gave my best. Sometimes it was good enough to win and sometimes not. Regardless, I always gave my best. I would like to acknowledge Jeffrey Brucculeri, one of my coauthors, the real sportsman among us. His contribution to this book reinforces the wise adage … "Good, better, best; never let it rest until your good is better and your better is best."

~ Richard Possett

I must begin by thanking my wife, Colleen, and our children, Joshua and Alyssa, for their patience, and for allowing me the time I needed to sit down and write my portion of this book. Also, thanks to my coauthors who were gracious enough to let me be a part of this project.

~ Jeffrey Brucculeri

The Discourse

When we speak of being powerful, we mean that in the most positive sense. We're not talking about using your power to control others and force them to do things your way. Our definition of power is synonymous with *being a positive influence* or *having the ability and wherewithal to achieve success in all aspects of your life.* It's empowering to know we've done our best, we've achieved our goals, and we've helped others along the way.

One of the speeches I deliver to groups and organizations is entitled, *The 5 Ds to Dynamic Living: Desire, Determination, Dedication, Discipline, and Deity.* In that speech I talk about how everything begins with desire. Without the desire to do something we would never do or be anything. A baby takes his first steps because he has the desire to "come to momma." In this book we address taking those first steps toward your personal success.

Determination means having a bulldog's attitude that you're going to get out of the yard no matter what, even if you have to drag the doghouse with you. As Jim Valvano said at the ESPY Awards, "Don't give up, don't ever give up." Keep going until your reach your goals, then set new ones and keep on going.

One definition of dedication is *the act of binding yourself (intellectually and emotionally) to a particular course of action.* That's total devotion to a particular cause or outcome. Are you totally dedicated to achieving whatever it is that you want to accomplish in life?

Being disciplined means a regimen or training to produce a desired outcome. In other words, practice, practice, practice. To improve their hitting, baseball players spend countless hours in the batting cage. Golfers who want to improve their score spend a lot of time on the putting green and the driving range. Basketball players shoot hundreds of baskets each day to improve their accuracy. In this same manner you can continue to train and practice your profession, whatever it might be. I'm a firm believer in continuing to educate ourselves even after we think we've arrived. Reading, listening to informational and educational CDs, and attending seminars are just a few ways you practice the discipline it takes to improve.

And the final "d" stands for deity. Not to get preachy here, but I believe without spiritual fulfillment (a relationship with God) we may obtain success, but our spirits remain empty. So to nourish the three core characteristics of being human (body, mind and spirit) and to be truly healthy, we must exercise and eat right to care for our body, we must educate our minds, and we must have spiritual communication with our Creator.

These are the principles set forth in this book, and we hope through theses practices you will not only achieve a powerful lifestyle, but one that is also very dynamic and rewarding.

~ Jeffrey Brucculeri

Introduction

What (or Who) Is a Powerful Athlete?

By definition athletes are sportspersons. They are individuals, young and old, who participate in the games, the matches, the bouts, and the races, whether they are casual, devoted amateurs or professional athletes. The true athlete will strive to reach the pinnacle in his sport at his level of play. The powerful athlete will not only play the game with zeal, but influence others to do the same. Powerful athletes have broad perspectives. They not only play a good game, but they live a good life. They have passion, but also compassion. They have a comprehensive conception of the world. Theirs is a world of physical exercise, intellectual activity, proactive civic life, and fellowship. Powerful athletes are very effective in helping their communities by contributing their talents and resources to build youth sports facilities, visiting fans who are ill, and donating their time to reading programs and other charitable activities. They are coaches who uncover raw talent, who instruct and inspire young people to become not only better athletes but also better citizens. These athletes are powerful because they care about people, tend to their families, are concerned about their communities, and are dedicated to being the best they can be in their sport and as people.

What (or Who) Is a Powerful Person?

A powerful person is anyone who has influence over another person. Notice that we said *influence*, not *control*. Many people misunderstand power as a control issue. Whether you know it or not, you influence many people every day. It may be as obvious as your interaction with a coworker or a family member or as subtle as your mannerisms when standing in a long checkout line at the store. In every circumstance, especially on the job, where you can be observed by others, you are exerting influence by your words and actions. As a powerful person, you influence everyone with whom you come in contact. The more powerful you are as a person, the more powerful your influence will become. The more powerful your influence is, the more lives you will be able to touch and change.

This book will address the characteristics that you show to the people in your life. These are the same characteristics that these same people look at when determining how powerful a person you are to them. The powerful people quoted in this book were powerful because of their influence on others, even you. You may never have met any one of these individuals, just as you may not have met many of the people that you have affected, either positively or negatively.

In the margin of this page take a minute now to list the most powerful influences in your life, especially other people who have influenced you the most. This is where your powerful lifestyle example begins.

How to Use This Book

Every day you are given the opportunity to be more proficient in a skill that leads you to become a more powerful person. Read the daily quotation and then thoughtfully complete the task presented. You may need more room to write your answers in many of the assignments and will perhaps want to reflect further on many others. Therefore, a daily journal will be very helpful or just use additional paper. By following through with these exercises you will become a more powerful person.

Six Months Review

The six months review gives you the opportunity to add depth to what you have learned and to the task that you had started, and hopefully completed, earlier. This is critical to ensure that good habits, not just actions, are created and reinforced. At the end, you will find that you have addressed all of the major areas that make you a more powerful person.

To reinforce certain key points, you may see a topic covered more than once. Note that this is a key topic requiring your thorough and honest attention.

Sample Illustration

JANUARY 1

JULY 1

Anyone who stops learning is old, whether at twenty or eighty. Anyone who keeps learning stays young.

~ Henry Ford

Note the names of two people that you know who seem to have remained young regardless of their years. Contact them for a meeting to discuss learning. During the meeting ask them how they have managed to remain young.

Name: *Albert Youngman*

Action: *Telephone Al to schedule a luncheon meeting to discuss his views on learning and staying young.*

Name: *Maria Youthful*

Action: *Talk with Maria at church and set-up a meeting with her to explore how she continues to stay young through her desire to continue learning.*

SIX MONTHS REVIEW:

I had lunch with Al, and he feels that learning is a lifelong quest for new ideas. Remaining open to new ideas has kept him on the cutting edge and feeling youthful. I met with Maria and she believes that one cannot teach without keeping up with how it feels to learn. That passion for learning is then communicated to her students and their youthful exuberance is shared with her and keeps her young.

QUOTATION SOURCE INFORMATION:

Credited with inventing the automobile or at least the assembly line to manufacture the auto more efficiently and at a lower cost, Ford continued to learn and study new things all the way up to his death.

About the Quote Sources

If you desire to receive further rewards from the assignments, do detailed research on the people quoted on the daily exercise pages in this book. You are encouraged to learn about their unique lives and special times. Learning how these individuals became power-driven people in their own right can be fascinating and educational. If someone happens to be quoted more than once, research the circumstances surrounding the passage. In the instances of sayings and proverbs, a study into the traditions associated with each aphorism may be instructive. Consider doing the same for the unknown authors. Getting to know the composer of the quotation and the particulars surrounding the passages can be a meaningful journey into history. The results of your study and research can be placed in the lines provided, which are labeled as "Quotation Source Information." Here we have an important announcement: Please understand that in instances in which a quotation or manuscript text refers to "him," the word "her" can simply be substituted.

And please remember …

"The wisdom of the wise, and the experience of the ages, may be preserved by quotation."

~ Benjamin Disraeli

And we say …

Tell me … I'll forget

Show me … I'll remember

Involve me … I'll comprehend

Be great but get better!

Be a Powerful Person!

JANUARY 1
JULY 2

When pride comes, then comes disgrace, but with humility comes wisdom.

~ Solomon

Big money, big accomplishments, big head! Do you have a problem with pride?
_____

Name some ways in which you can gain humility and wisdom each day.

1. _____
   _____

2. _____
   _____

3. _____
   _____

SIX MONTHS REVIEW:

_____
_____
_____

QUOTATION SOURCE INFORMATION:

_____
_____
_____

January 2

July 3

Everything begins with desire. Without the desire to do something, you would never do or be anything.

~ Jeffrey Brucculeri

List several activities that you've always wanted to do, places you've wanted to visit, and goals you've wanted to achieve.

_____

_____

_____

How can you complete each of these visions for your life?

_____

_____

_____

_____

Six Months Review:

_____

_____

_____

Quotation Source Information:

_____

_____

_____

JANUARY 3

JULY 4

If you don't do what's best for your body, you're the one who comes up on the short end.

~ Julius Erving

Determine in your mind three things you can do, starting now, to improve your health.

1. _____

2. _____

3. _____

SIX MONTHS REVIEW:

_____
_____
_____

QUOTATION SOURCE INFORMATION:

_____
_____
_____

January 4

July 5

If you set a goal for yourself and are able to achieve it, you have won your race. Your goal can be to come in first, to improve your performance, or just finish the race. It's up to you.

~ Dave Scott

What three goals do you want to accomplish this year?

1. _____

2. _____

3. _____

List the activities needed to accomplish each goal.

1. _____
   _____

2. _____
   _____

3. _____
   _____

SIX MONTHS REVIEW:

_____

_____

_____

QUOTATION SOURCE INFORMATION:

_____

_____

_____

January 5

July 6

The principle is competing against yourself. It's about self-improvement, and about being better than you were the day before.

~ Steve Young

In what three areas of your life do you want to improve and in what way?

1. _____

_____

_____

2. _____

_____

_____

3. _____

_____

_____

SIX MONTHS REVIEW:

_____

_____

_____

QUOTATION SOURCE INFORMATION:

_____

_____

_____

January 6

July 7

I am not a role model.

~ Charles Barkley

Name three people in your life who have been positive role models to you.
Write down how they've inspired you, then contact them and let them know.

1. _____

   _____

   _____

2. _____

   _____

   _____

3. _____

   _____

   _____

Six Months Review:

_____

_____

_____

Quotation Source Information:

_____

_____

_____

January 7

July 8

Ability is what you're capable of doing. Motivation determines what you do. Attitude determines how well you do it.

~ Lou Holtz

What are your abilities?

_____

_____

_____

What motivates you?

_____

_____

_____

Check your attitude. Do you need an attitude adjustment?

_____

SIX MONTHS REVIEW:

_____

_____

_____

QUOTATION SOURCE INFORMATION:

_____

_____

_____

January 8

July 9

You have no control over what the other guy does. You only have control over what you do.

~ A. J. Kitt

List three items that you have delayed or procrastinated in doing.

1. _____

_____

2. _____

_____

3. _____

_____

Next to each uncompleted task listed, write one thing you will do today to begin to accomplish the task.

Make a plan to complete each task and DO IT!

_____

_____

_____

_____

SIX MONTHS REVIEW:

_____

_____

_____

QUOTATION SOURCE INFORMATION:

_____

_____

_____

January 9
July 10

You learn you can do your best even when it's hard, even when you're tired and maybe hurting a little bit. It feels good to show some courage.

~ Joe Namath

Describe a time in your life that was tough and how you overcame it.

_____
_____
_____
_____

Describe what you can do to overcome any future tough times and how you can help others to be courageous.

_____
_____
_____
_____

Six Months Review:

_____
_____
_____

Quotation Source Information:

_____
_____
_____

January 10
July 11

It doesn't matter who scores the points, it's who can get the ball to the scorer.

~ Larry Bird

List specific ways that you can help others achieve their goals.

1. _____

_____

2. _____

_____

3. _____

_____

Six Months Review:

_____

_____

_____

Quotation Source Information:

_____

_____

_____

January 11
July 12

I'm a great believer in luck, and I find the harder I work, the more I have of it.

~ Thomas Jefferson

What can you do today to create some breaks for yourself and your career?

_____

_____

_____

_____

Who can you call that may be able to help open some doors for you?

_____

_____

Six Months Review:

_____

_____

_____

Quotation Source Information:

_____

_____

_____

January 12

July 13

Before you can win a game, you have to not lose it.

~ Chuck Noll

How does winning make you feel?

_____

_____

_____

How do you feel when you lose?

_____

_____

_____

Six Months Review:

_____

_____

_____

Quotation Source Information:

_____

_____

_____

JANUARY 13

JULY 14

What is the worst thing that can happen to a quarterback? He loses his confidence.

~ Terry Bradshaw

What is it that shakes your confidence?

_____

_____

_____

List three ways you can gain more confidence.

1. _____

2. _____

3. _____

SIX MONTHS REVIEW:

_____

_____

_____

QUOTATION SOURCE INFORMATION:

_____

_____

_____

JANUARY 14
JULY 15

Running is cheap therapy.

~ Peter Biadasz

Not only is exercise a great stress reliever, but it helps improve your physical health. List your favorite physical activities.

_____

_____

_____

_____

_____

Make a commitment to "get physical" at least three times a week.

SIX MONTHS REVIEW:

_____

_____

_____

QUOTATION SOURCE INFORMATION:

_____

_____

_____

JANUARY 15

JULY 16

When you're playing for the national championship, it's not a matter of life or death. It's more important than that.

~ Duffy Daugherty

Are there things in your life that are more important than life or death? _____

Should they be that important? _____

What issues seem to be more important than life and death to you?

_____

_____

_____

_____

SIX MONTHS REVIEW:

_____

_____

_____

QUOTATION SOURCE INFORMATION:

_____

_____

_____

January 16
July 17

It's what you learn after you know it all that counts.

~ John Wooden

What books have you read that have strongly influenced you?

1. _____

2. _____

3. _____

How can you share the influence of those books with others?

_____

_____

_____

_____

Six Months Review:

_____

_____

_____

Quotation Source Information:

_____

_____

_____

JANUARY 17

JULY 18

Ask not what your teammates can do for you. Ask what you can do for your teammates.

~ Ervin "Magic" Johnson

In what ways are you a great motivator or team player?

1. _____

2. _____

3. _____

SIX MONTHS REVIEW:

_____

_____

QUOTATION SOURCE INFORMATION:

_____

_____

JANUARY 18

JULY 19

A "try" in the sport of rugby is a score. A "try" in the game of life is a start. In the former, we achieve. In the latter, we attempt.

~ Richard Possett

Success in life means getting things done and not merely trying. Of course, let's not be afraid to try but don't lose sight of the goal. What was your last failure? What have you done to make it a scoring success?

_____

_____

_____

_____

_____

_____

_____

SIX MONTHS REVIEW:

_____

_____

_____

QUOTATION SOURCE INFORMATION:

_____

_____

_____

JANUARY 19
JULY 20

Luck is what happens when preparation meets opportunity.

~ Seneca

Record three opportunities that are available to you right now.

1. _____

   _____

2. _____

   _____

3. _____

   _____

What will you do today to capitalize on each of these opportunities?

_____

_____

_____

SIX MONTHS REVIEW:

_____

_____

_____

QUOTATION SOURCE INFORMATION:

_____

_____

_____

JANUARY 20

JULY 21

When you're riding, only the race in which you're riding is important.

~ Bill Shoemaker

How can you improve your focus?

1. _____

_____

2. _____

_____

3. _____

_____

SIX MONTHS REVIEW:

_____

_____

_____

QUOTATION SOURCE INFORMATION:

_____

_____

_____

January 21

July 22

If at first you don't succeed, you are running about average.

~ M. H. Alderson

In what five areas of your life could you raise your standards, and what can you do today to improve your standards in each area?

1. _____

2. _____

3. _____

4. _____

5. _____

SIX MONTHS REVIEW:

_____

_____

_____

QUOTATION SOURCE INFORMATION:

_____

_____

_____

JANUARY 22
JULY 23

I really lack the words to compliment myself today.

~ Alberto Tomba

Name five things that you do very well.

1. _____

2. _____

3. _____

4. _____

5. _____

SIX MONTHS REVIEW:

_____

_____

_____

QUOTATION SOURCE INFORMATION:

_____

_____

_____

JANUARY 23

JULY 24

There are only two options regarding commitment. You're either in or you're out. There is no such thing as life in-between.

~ Pat Riley

To what things in your life are you totally committed?

_____

_____

_____

_____

What things are you not committed to that need to be eliminated?

_____

_____

_____

_____

SIX MONTHS REVIEW:

_____

_____

_____

QUOTATION SOURCE INFORMATION:

_____

_____

_____

January 24

July 25

Adversity causes some men to break; others to break records.

~ William A. Ward

How can adversity educate you?

1. _____
2. _____
3. _____
4. _____

How do you pass those lessons on to your coworkers or teammates?

_____

_____

_____

SIX MONTHS REVIEW:

_____

_____

_____

QUOTATION SOURCE INFORMATION:

_____

_____

_____

January 25

July 26

There is no substitute for guts.

~ Paul "Bear" Bryant

Think about and record ways in which you've shown a lot of "guts."

1. _____

_____

2. _____

_____

3. _____

_____

SIX MONTHS REVIEW:

_____

_____

_____

QUOTATION SOURCE INFORMATION:

_____

_____

_____

January 26
July 27

To succeed, you need to find something to hold on to, something to motivate you, something to inspire you.

~ Tony Dorsett

List the person in each category who has inspired you the most and describe how each one inspired you.

Family: _____

_____

Teacher: _____

_____

Coach: _____

_____

Colleague: _____

_____

Inspire others in your life by following the examples of the people you listed!

SIX MONTHS REVIEW:

_____

_____

_____

QUOTATION SOURCE INFORMATION:

_____

_____

_____

January 27

July 28

Set your goals high, and don't stop till you get there.

~ Bo Jackson

Write your goals for improving your skills and your plans for getting better at what you do.

1. _____
   _____

2. _____
   _____

3. _____
   _____

SIX MONTHS REVIEW:

_____
_____
_____

QUOTATION SOURCE INFORMATION:

_____
_____
_____

JANUARY 28

JULY 29

The best and fastest way to learn a sport is to watch and imitate a champion.

~ Jean-Claude Killy

Name the people who have taken you on an exciting expedition of discovery and write how each person motivated you.

1. _____

_____

2. _____

_____

3. _____

_____

SIX MONTHS REVIEW:

_____

_____

_____

QUOTATION SOURCE INFORMATION:

_____

_____

_____

JANUARY 29
JULY 30

If you can believe it, the mind can achieve it.

~ Ronnie Lott

How do you keep yourself motivated?

_____

_____

_____

What are you thinking about right now that you want to achieve?

_____

_____

_____

How can you teach others to keep themselves motivated?

_____

_____

_____

SIX MONTHS REVIEW:

_____

_____

_____

QUOTATION SOURCE INFORMATION:

_____

_____

_____

January 30

July 31

I've always made a total effort, even when the odds seemed entirely against me. I never quit trying; I never felt that I didn't have a chance to win.

~ Arnold Palmer

What are three common excuses for quitting that you use when problems arise?

1. _____

2. _____

3. _____

How can each excuse be dismissed and conquered?

1. _____

2. _____

3. _____

SIX MONTHS REVIEW:

_____

_____

_____

QUOTATION SOURCE INFORMATION:

_____

_____

_____

JANUARY 31
AUGUST 1

Genius is one percent inspiration and ninety-nine percent perspiration.

~ Thomas Edison

What qualities are most important for a powerful person to possess?

1. _____

2. _____

3. _____

How can you further develop these qualities in yourself?

_____

_____

SIX MONTHS REVIEW:

_____

_____

QUOTATION SOURCE INFORMATION:

_____

_____

February 1
August 2

It's a little like wrestling a gorilla. You don't quit when you're tired, you quit when the gorilla is tired.

~ Robert Strauss

Either we beat our circumstances or the circumstances overtake us. What is one thing in your life that consistently seems to beat you down?

_____

_____

_____

List the steps required to beat this "gorilla" into submission.

1. _____

_____

2. _____

_____

3. _____

_____

Six Months Review:

_____

_____

_____

Quotation Source Information:

_____

_____

_____

FEBRUARY 2

AUGUST 3

You need to play with supreme confidence, or else you'll lose again, and then losing becomes a habit.

~ Joe Paterno

How do you light a fire within yourself?

_____

_____

_____

How do you light a fire within others?

_____

_____

_____

SIX MONTHS REVIEW:

_____

_____

_____

QUOTATION SOURCE INFORMATION:

_____

_____

_____

February 3
August 4

You have to expect things of yourself before you can do them.

~ Michael Jordan

Enthusiasm can be very contagious. How can you increase your enthusiasm?

_____

_____

_____

How can you increase the enthusiasm of those with whom you work?

_____

_____

_____

Six Months Review:

_____

_____

_____

Quotation Source Information:

_____

_____

_____

AUGUST 5

Being an influence to others happens. Being a positive influence takes work.

~ Jeffrey Brucculeri

Name three athletes you admire because of the way they teach by example. Write down how they've influenced you.

1. _____
_____
_____

2. _____
_____
_____

3. _____
_____
_____

SIX MONTHS REVIEW:

_____
_____
_____

QUOTATION SOURCE INFORMATION:

_____
_____
_____

FEBRUARY 5

AUGUST 6

To be prepared is half the victory.

~ Miguel Cervantes

Preparation is the key to success. How can you prepare to meet your challenges on a daily basis?

1. _____

_____

2. _____

_____

3. _____

_____

What are ways others you respect prepare for their battles?

1. _____

_____

2. _____

_____

3. _____

_____

SIX MONTHS REVIEW:

_____

_____

_____

QUOTATION SOURCE INFORMATION:

_____

_____

_____

FEBRUARY 6

AUGUST 7

The best physical performance comes as a result of the best mental preparation.

~ Peter Biadasz

How do you prepare mentally to ensure you perform at your physical best?

_____

_____

_____

_____

How can you take this preparation to a new and higher level?

_____

_____

_____

SIX MONTHS REVIEW:

_____

_____

_____

QUOTATION SOURCE INFORMATION:

_____

_____

_____

FEBRUARY 7

AUGUST 8

Each warrior wants to leave the mark of his will, his signature, on important acts he touches. This is not the voice of ego but of the human spirit, rising up and declaring that it has something to contribute to the solution of the hardest problems, no matter how vexing!

~ Pat Riley

What do you want your legacy to be? How do you want to be remembered when you're gone?

_____

_____

_____

_____

_____

_____

SIX MONTHS REVIEW:

_____

_____

_____

QUOTATION SOURCE INFORMATION:

_____

_____

_____

February 8

August 9

I'll always be Number 1 to myself.

~ Moses Malone

List five things that you truly like about yourself.

1. _____
2. _____
3. _____
4. _____
5. _____

How does it make you feel to read that list?

_____

_____

_____

Six Months Review:

_____

_____

_____

Quotation Source Information:

_____

_____

_____

FEBRUARY 9
AUGUST 10

Ingenuity, plus courage, plus work, equals miracles.

~ Bob Richards

Make a list of practical applications of the meaning of this quotation.

1. _____

_____

2. _____

_____

3. _____

_____

4. _____

_____

SIX MONTHS REVIEW:

_____

_____

_____

QUOTATION SOURCE INFORMATION:

_____

_____

_____

FEBRUARY 10

AUGUST 11

The difference between a successful person and others is not a lack of strength, not a lack of knowledge, but rather a lack of will.

~ Vince Lombardi

How do you make opportunities, and how do you take advantage of them?

1. _____
   _____

2. _____
   _____

3. _____
   _____

How can you teach others to make opportunities for themselves?

_____

_____

_____

SIX MONTHS REVIEW:

_____

_____

_____

QUOTATION SOURCE INFORMATION:

_____

_____

_____

FEBRUARY 11

AUGUST 12

The winners in life think constantly in terms of I can, I will, and I am. Losers, on the other hand, concentrate their waking thoughts on what they should have or would have done, or what they can't do.

~ Denis Waitley

How are your thoughts controlling your life?

_____

_____

_____

What can you do right now so you don't regret not doing it later?

_____

_____

_____

SIX MONTHS REVIEW:

_____

_____

_____

QUOTATION SOURCE INFORMATION:

_____

_____

_____

AUGUST 13

**It's lack of faith that makes people afraid of meeting challenges,
and I believed in myself.**

~ Muhammad Ali

Do you believe in yourself? _____ Keep a record of ways you can improve
your self-respect.

1. _____

_____

2. _____

_____

3. _____

_____

How can you pass these lessons on to your coworkers or teammates?

_____

_____

_____

_____

SIX MONTHS REVIEW:

_____

_____

_____

QUOTATION SOURCE INFORMATION:

_____

_____

_____

February 13

August 14

Sweat plus sacrifice equals success.

~ Charlie O. Finley

What things do you do daily to ensure your success as a person and as a professional?

1. _____

_____

2. _____

_____

3. _____

_____

How can you teach these practices to those around you?

_____

_____

_____

SIX MONTHS REVIEW:

_____

_____

_____

QUOTATION SOURCE INFORMATION:

_____

_____

_____

FEBRUARY 14

AUGUST 15

Do not let what you cannot do interfere with what you can do.

~ John Wooden

In what areas do you know you are not performing at your best?

1. _____

2. _____

3. _____

Formulate a plan to reach your full potential in each area listed.

_____

_____

_____

_____

SIX MONTHS REVIEW:

_____

_____

_____

QUOTATION SOURCE INFORMATION:

_____

_____

_____

February 15

August 16

The difference between the impossible and the possible lies in a man's determination.

~ Tommy Lasorda

Name three people who show determination in all that they do.

1. _____
2. _____
3. _____

Talk with each person to learn his secret to determination.

SIX MONTHS REVIEW:

_____
_____
_____

QUOTATION SOURCE INFORMATION:

_____
_____
_____

FEBRUARY 16

AUGUST 17

Did you know that the most famous line in the American national anthem is … "play ball"?

~ Richard Possett

Sports and patriotism have been interrelated throughout the history of the man. Just look at the Olympic Games and consider the financial and human resources that are allocated to this significant sporting event every four years. We would have it no other way. In the space provided below, note how sports personally affect your life.

_____

_____

_____

_____

_____

_____

SIX MONTHS REVIEW:

_____

_____

_____

QUOTATION SOURCE INFORMATION:

_____

_____

_____

FEBRUARY 17

AUGUST 18

I know that I'm never as good or bad as any single performance. I've never believed my critics or my [worshipers], and I've always been able to leave the game at the arena.

~ Charles Barkley

Describe how you can learn from this quotation. Are you humble? Do you let your critics get you down? Are you able to leave your work at the "office"?

_____

_____

_____

_____

_____

_____

Begin implementing these ideas this week.

SIX MONTHS REVIEW:

_____

_____

_____

QUOTATION SOURCE INFORMATION:

_____

_____

_____

FEBRUARY 18

AUGUST 19

When you're in the back of the pack, you can gamble a little bit more.

~ Michael Andretti

Taking calculated risks is a very important part of any success. Name three times when you took necessary risks to achieve success.

1. _____
   _____

2. _____
   _____

3. _____
   _____

Record above what you learned from each experience.

SIX MONTHS REVIEW:

_____
_____
_____

QUOTATION SOURCE INFORMATION:

_____
_____
_____

February 19

August 20

Concentration is the ability to think about absolutely nothing when it is absolutely necessary.

~ Ray Knight

To be truly excellent at anything one must perform a task, any task, without conscious effort. List the things at which you are the best that require little or no mental effort.

1. _____

_____

2. _____

_____

3. _____

_____

Be grateful for these areas of expertise.

Six Months Review:

_____

_____

_____

Quotation Source Information:

_____

_____

_____

FEBRUARY 20

AUGUST 21

The game isn't over 'til it's over.

~ Lawrence "Yogi" Berra

List three things you would like to do before you die (let your imagination go and dream big).

1. _____

2. _____

3. _____

SIX MONTHS REVIEW:

_____
_____
_____

QUOTATION SOURCE INFORMATION:

_____
_____
_____

FEBRUARY 21
AUGUST 22

A wise person decides slowly but abides by these decisions.

~ Arthur Ashe

Anyone can make a quick uninformed decision. A wise person looks at every angle of a situation then makes a decision he can live with for a lifetime. How can you ensure all your decisions are made as a wise person?

_____

_____

_____

_____

_____

_____

SIX MONTHS REVIEW:

_____

_____

_____

QUOTATION SOURCE INFORMATION:

_____

_____

_____

FEBRUARY 22

AUGUST 23

If you train hard, you will not only be hard, you'll be hard to beat.

~ Herschel Walker

List ways you can train harder.

1. _____
   _____

2. _____
   _____

3. _____
   _____

SIX MONTHS REVIEW:

_____
_____
_____

QUOTATION SOURCE INFORMATION:

_____
_____
_____

February 23
August 24

When someone tells me there is only one way to do things, it always lights a fire under my butt. My instant reaction is, I'm gonna prove you wrong.

~ Picabo Street

How does the above quotation inspire you?

_____

_____

_____

In what ways have you proven people wrong?

_____

_____

_____

SIX MONTHS REVIEW:

_____

_____

_____

QUOTATION SOURCE INFORMATION:

_____

_____

_____

February 24
August 25

I always felt that my greatest asset was not my physical ability, it was my mental ability.

~ Bruce Jenner

Are you continuing to learn? _____

List learning opportunities of which you have taken advantage lately or learning opportunities of which you are going to take advantage.

1. _____
_____

2. _____
_____

3. _____
_____

Six Months Review:

_____
_____
_____

Quotation Source Information:

_____
_____
_____

February 25

August 26

Don't look back. Something might be gaining on you.

~ Satchel Paige

What are your biggest fears?

1. _____

_____

2. _____

_____

3. _____

_____

Do each of the things that you fear TODAY and brag to someone about conquering that fear.

SIX MONTHS REVIEW:

_____

_____

_____

QUOTATION SOURCE INFORMATION:

_____

_____

_____

February 26

August 27

I define fear as standing across the ring from Joe Louis and knowing he wants to go home early.

~ Max Baer

Fear! We all experience it at some time or another. Describe your greatest fears.

1. _____
   _____

2. _____
   _____

3. _____
   _____

In the space next to each fear listed, describe a plan to overcome that fear.

Six Months Review:

_____
_____
_____

Quotation Source Information:

_____
_____
_____

FEBRUARY 27

AUGUST 28

The man who can drive himself further once the effort gets painful is the man who will win.

~ Roger Bannister

We all have experienced the pain of growth. How do you work comfortably in uncomfortable circumstances?

_____

_____

_____

_____

_____

_____

SIX MONTHS REVIEW:

_____

_____

_____

QUOTATION SOURCE INFORMATION:

_____

_____

_____

FEBRUARY 28

AUGUST 29

If you chase two rabbits, both will escape.

~ Unknown

Very rarely, if ever, can you be an expert in two difficult areas. How can you ensure you are truly pursuing your passions with singleness of purpose?

_____

_____

_____

_____

_____

_____

_____

SIX MONTHS REVIEW:

_____

_____

_____

FEBRUARY 29

AUGUST 30

In war there is no substitute for victory.

~ Douglas MacArthur

If you lose a war, you may die, literally. How can you guarantee, to the best of your ability, that you will always be victorious in any endeavor you undertake?

1. _____

_____

2. _____

_____

3. _____

_____

SIX MONTHS REVIEW:

_____

_____

_____

QUOTATION SOURCE INFORMATION:

_____

_____

_____

MARCH 1

AUGUST 31

You have to perform at a consistently higher level than others.
That's the mark of a true professional.

~ Joe Paterno

Describe yourself in your role as a professional.

_____

_____

_____

_____

_____

_____

SIX MONTHS REVIEW:

_____

_____

_____

QUOTATION SOURCE INFORMATION:

_____

_____

_____

March 2

September 1

The minute you start talking about what you're going to do if you lose, you have lost.

~ George Schultz

Describe how you can begin to think more positively.

_____

_____

_____

_____

_____

_____

Six Months Review:

_____

_____

Quotation Source Information:

_____

_____

_____

MARCH 3

SEPTEMBER 2

Don't give up. Don't ever give up.

~ Jim Valvano

Jim Valvano made this statement while giving a speech, knowing he was dying of brain cancer. How can you use his example to inspire your life?

_____

_____

_____

_____

_____

_____

SIX MONTHS REVIEW:

_____

_____

_____

QUOTATION SOURCE INFORMATION:

_____

_____

_____

MARCH 4

SEPTEMBER 3

Perhaps the single most important element in mastering the techniques and tactics of racing is experience. But once you have the fundamentals, acquiring the experience is a matter of time.

~ Greg LeMond

How do you master the fundamentals of your profession?

_____

_____

_____

List three of the most critical fundamentals.

1. _____
2. _____
3. _____

SIX MONTHS REVIEW:

_____

_____

_____

QUOTATION SOURCE INFORMATION:

_____

_____

_____

March 5

September 4

I learned that if you want to make it bad enough, no matter how bad it is, you can make it.

~ Gale Sayers

What do you want so badly that no matter what, you won't quit until you get it?

1. _____

   _____

2. _____

   _____

3. _____

   _____

Six Months Review:

_____

_____

_____

Quotation Source Information:

_____

_____

_____

March 6

September 5

You have to decide that you're going to be successful before you'll ever become successful.

~ Jeffrey Brucculeri

Have you decided to become successful? _____

List three reasons why you want to be successful.

1. _____

_____

2. _____

_____

3. _____

_____

Six Months Review:

_____

_____

_____

Quotation Source Information:

_____

_____

_____

March 7

September 6

Things turn out best for people who make the best out of the way things turn out.

~ John Wooden

Just because things may not turn out the way you thought they might does not make an experience bad. Sometimes unexpected pleasures result from unexpected occurrences. What are some ways you can make the best out of any circumstance?

1. _____

   _____

2. _____

   _____

3. _____

   _____

Six Months Review:

_____

_____

_____

Quotation Source Information:

_____

_____

_____

March 8

September 7

The first time I perform in public is not the first time I have performed as if in public.

~ Peter Biadasz

In any endeavor, preparation is key to maximum performance. List some ways to ensure your practice habits are as strong as your desired performance.

1. _____

_____

2. _____

_____

3. _____

_____

Six Months Review:

_____

_____

_____

Quotation Source Information:

_____

_____

_____

March 9
September 8

Show me a guy who's afraid to look bad, and I'll show you a guy you can beat every time.

~ Lou Brock

Oftentimes people confuse looking good with performing well. At times the best performance may not be the prettiest. How can you guarantee your priorities produce your best effort?

1. _____

2. _____

3. _____

Six Months Review:

_____

_____

_____

Quotation Source Information:

_____

_____

_____

March 10

September 9

The price of success is hard work, dedication to the job at hand, and the determination that whether we win or lose, we have applied the best of ourselves to the task at hand.

~ Vince Lombardi

In what areas do you feel that you have unused potential?

1. _____

2. _____

3. _____

Write an action plan to utilize your unused potential in each area.

1. _____
   _____

2. _____
   _____

3. _____
   _____

Six Months Review:

_____

_____

_____

Quotation Source Information:

_____

_____

_____

MARCH 11

SEPTEMBER 10

We cannot know work without play, for we work to survive and play for sport.

~ Richard Possett

In what sports are you engaged as a source of diversion from your work and as a way of staying physically and mentally healthy?

1. _____
2. _____
3. _____

SIX MONTHS REVIEW:

_____
_____
_____

QUOTATION SOURCE INFORMATION:

_____
_____
_____

March 12

September 11

Whatever you do, don't do it halfway.

~ Bob Beamon

Dedication is a common attribute among successful people. Name the most dedicated people to whom you have been exposed.

1. _____
2. _____
3. _____

What defines the dedication of each person listed?

1. _____
2. _____
3. _____

Six Months Review:

_____

_____

_____

Quotation Source Information:

_____

_____

_____

March 13

September 12

The way a team plays as a whole determines its success. You may have the greatest bunch of individual stars in the world, but if they don't play together, the club won't be worth a dime.

~ Babe Ruth

We are often so preoccupied with our individual performance that we forget to consider the team concept. How can you ensure you are performing at your best while guaranteeing you are a strong contributing member of the team?

1. _____
   _____
2. _____
   _____
3. _____
   _____

SIX MONTHS REVIEW:

_____
_____
_____

QUOTATION SOURCE INFORMATION:

_____
_____
_____

March 14
September 13

I love my family.

~ Manute Bol

What a strong statement spoken by a successful man. What is your first love?

_____

_____

_____

How can you be confident your priority is correct with regard to your first love?

_____

_____

_____

SIX MONTHS REVIEW:

_____

_____

_____

QUOTATION SOURCE INFORMATION:

_____

_____

_____

MARCH 15
SEPTEMBER 14

How you respond to the challenge in the second half will determine what you become after the game, whether you are a winner or a loser.

~ Lou Holtz

Your true character is reflected when you are tired and facing a challenge. How can you improve the way you respond to adversity, especially when tired or fatigued?

1. _____
   _____
2. _____
   _____
3. _____
   _____

SIX MONTHS REVIEW:

_____
_____
_____

QUOTATION SOURCE INFORMATION:

_____
_____
_____

MARCH 16

SEPTEMBER 15

It's not the size of the dog in the fight, but the size of the fight in the dog.

~ Mark Twain

Being successful at anything and being a good leader take courage. In your hierarchy of leadership qualities, where do you place courage and why?

_____

_____

_____

_____

_____

_____

SIX MONTHS REVIEW:

_____

_____

_____

QUOTATION SOURCE INFORMATION:

_____

_____

_____

MARCH 17

SEPTEMBER 16

My motto was always to keep swinging. Whether I was in a slump or feeling badly or having trouble off the field, the only thing to do was keep swinging.

~ Henry Aaron

Perseverance separates the winners from the true champions. How do those you admire maintain a champion's mindset even when not performing at their highest levels?

1. _____
   _____
2. _____
   _____
3. _____
   _____

SIX MONTHS REVIEW:

_____
_____
_____

QUOTATION SOURCE INFORMATION:

_____
_____
_____

MARCH 18
SEPTEMBER 17

The will to win is important, but the will to prepare is vital.

~ Joe Paterno

List skills you want to improve.

1. _____
2. _____
3. _____

Formulate an action plan to improve each skill.

1. _____
_____
2. _____
_____
3. _____
_____

SIX MONTHS REVIEW:

_____
_____
_____

QUOTATION SOURCE INFORMATION:

_____
_____
_____

March 19
September 18

Great works are performed not by strength but by perseverance.

~ Samuel Johnson

How can you ensure maximum perseverance in your training and preparation habits?

_____

_____

_____

_____

_____

_____

Six Months Review:

_____

_____

_____

Quotation Source Information:

_____

_____

_____

March 20
September 19

Other people may not have had high expectations of me, but I had high expectations for myself.

~ Shannon Miller

The theory of self-fulfilling prophecy states that you will become what you expect, either positive or negative. How can you form high expectations of yourself and fulfill those desires?

1. _____

2. _____

3. _____

SIX MONTHS REVIEW:

_____

_____

_____

QUOTATION SOURCE INFORMATION:

_____

_____

_____

MARCH 21

SEPTEMBER 20

The country is full of good coaches. What it takes to win is a bunch of interested players.

~ Don Coryell

Coaches coach, players perform. What are the best examples of teamwork you are aware of in which the players being coached were the most interested in success as a unit?

1. _____

2. _____

3. _____

Who has helped you learn teamwork even in individual endeavors? What has that person taught you?

_____
_____
_____

SIX MONTHS REVIEW:

_____
_____
_____

QUOTATION SOURCE INFORMATION:

_____
_____
_____

March 22
September 21

Excellence is the gradual result of always striving to do better.

~ Pat Riley

In what areas of your life are you making improvements?

_____

_____

_____

_____

In what areas could you strive to do better?

_____

_____

_____

_____

Six Months Review:

_____

_____

_____

Quotation Source Information:

_____

_____

_____

March 23
September 22

Sports do not build character. They reveal it.

~ Haywood Hale Broun

What is your definition of character?

_____

_____

_____

What influences surround you that will better your character?

_____

_____

_____

Are there any negative character examples currently in your life? _____
If so, should they be in your life? Correct as appropriate.

SIX MONTHS REVIEW:

_____

_____

_____

QUOTATION SOURCE INFORMATION:

_____

_____

_____

March 24

September 23

What counts in sports is not the victory, but the magnificence of the struggle.

~ Joe Paterno

What struggles are you facing in your life right now and what can you learn from them?

_____

_____

_____

_____

_____

_____

_____

_____

Six Months Review:

_____

_____

_____

Quotation Source Information:

_____

_____

_____

March 25

September 24

Players win games, teams win championships.

~ Bill Taylor

List three things you have done where you worked with others and achieved a goal.

1. _____

   _____

2. _____

   _____

3. _____

   _____

Six Months Review:

_____

_____

_____

Quotation Source Information:

_____

_____

_____

MARCH 26

SEPTEMBER 25

The harder I practice, the luckier I get.

~ Gary Player

What is more important to you, hard work or luck? _____ Why?

_____

_____

Which can you control, your work ethic or luck?

_____

_____

How can you improve your work ethic?

_____

_____

SIX MONTHS REVIEW:

_____

_____

_____

QUOTATION SOURCE INFORMATION:

_____

_____

_____

MARCH 27

SEPTEMBER 26

We didn't lose the game; we just ran out of time.

~ Vince Lombardi

Preparation and time management go hand in hand. How can you improve your time management skills in all phases of your life?

1. _____

   _____

2. _____

   _____

3. _____

   _____

SIX MONTHS REVIEW:

_____

_____

_____

QUOTATION SOURCE INFORMATION:

_____

_____

_____

MARCH 28
SEPTEMBER 27

You gotta be a man to play baseball for a living, but you gotta have a lot of little boy in you, too.

~ Roy Campanella

How do you keep that little child in you alive?

_____

_____

_____

_____

Do something that you haven't done since you were a kid, and then describe how it makes you feel.

_____

_____

_____

_____

SIX MONTHS REVIEW:

_____

_____

_____

QUOTATION SOURCE INFORMATION:

_____

_____

_____

March 29

September 28

The strong take from the weak and the smart take from the strong.

~ Pete Carril

Remember hearing about the 1980 U.S. Olympic Hockey team? List instances in which the smarter and better prepared have been victorious over the stronger and better talented.

1. _____
2. _____
3. _____
4. _____
5. _____

Six Months Review:

_____
_____
_____

Quotation Source Information:

_____
_____
_____

March 30

September 29

You can discover more about a person in an hour of play than in a year of conversation.

~ Plato

Much business is done on the golf course because one can evaluate a person who faces a variety of challenges in a short amount of time. How do you consistently show your strongest attributes every time you "play"?

1. _____

   _____

2. _____

   _____

3. _____

   _____

SIX MONTHS REVIEW:

_____

_____

_____

QUOTATION SOURCE INFORMATION:

_____

_____

_____

March 31

September 30

I throw the ball as hard as ever, but it just takes longer to get to the plate.

~ Don Newcombe

As our careers advance, we all face challenges. Expressing humor is a great way to communicate our shortcomings gracefully. List ways in which humor has been an influence that assisted you in accepting your imperfections.

1. _____
   _____

2. _____
   _____

3. _____
   _____

SIX MONTHS REVIEW:

_____
_____
_____

QUOTATION SOURCE INFORMATION:

_____
_____
_____

APRIL 1

OCTOBER 1

I am more valuable to my team hitting .330 than swinging for home runs.

~ Roberto Clemente

What is more important to winning, individual performance or teamwork? Why?

_____

_____

_____

How can you improve in both areas?

_____

_____

_____

SIX MONTHS REVIEW:

_____

QUOTATION SOURCE INFORMATION:

_____

_____

_____

April 2

October 2

Not only is there more to life than basketball, there's a lot more to basketball than basketball.

~ Phil Jackson

What life lessons can you learn from your "sport"?

1. _____

2. _____

3. _____

How can you communicate these important lessons to others?

_____

_____

_____

SIX MONTHS REVIEW:

_____

_____

_____

QUOTATION SOURCE INFORMATION:

_____

_____

_____

April 3

October 3

There's a fine line between fishing and just standing on the shore like an idiot.

~ Steven Wright

Are you fishing for something? Are you constantly trying to catch something or are you just standing there watching? Explain.

_____

_____

_____

_____

_____

_____

Six Months Review:

_____

_____

_____

Quotation Source Information:

_____

_____

_____

APRIL 4

OCTOBER 4

Doctors and scientists said that breaking the four-minute mile was impossible, that one would die in the attempt. Thus, when I got up from the track after collapsing at the finish line, I figured I was dead.

~ Roger Bannister

What have you done that others have said was impossible?

_____

_____

_____

What do you want to do that right now is considered impossible?

_____

_____

_____

SIX MONTHS REVIEW:

_____

_____

_____

QUOTATION SOURCE INFORMATION:

_____

_____

_____

April 5

October 5

My dad has always taught me these words: care and share. That's why we put on clinics. The only thing I can do is try to give back. If it works, it works.

~ Tiger Woods

List some ways you can teach others and thereby give back in your community.

1. _____

_____

2. _____

_____

3. _____

_____

Six Months Review:

_____

_____

_____

Quotation Source Information:

_____

_____

_____

April 6

October 6

Champions keep playing until they get it right.

~ Billie Jean King

What is the relationship between discipline and perseverance?

_____

_____

Which is more important, discipline or perseverance? _____
Why?

_____

_____

What do you do to "get it right"?

_____

_____

Six Months Review:

_____

_____

_____

Quotation Source Information:

_____

_____

_____

APRIL 7

OCTOBER 7

Be more concerned with your character than your reputation, because your character is what you really are, while your reputation is merely what others think you are.

~ John Wooden

What are you doing to guarantee you are a person of outstanding character?

_____

_____

_____

_____

_____

_____

SIX MONTHS REVIEW:

_____

_____

_____

QUOTATION SOURCE INFORMATION:

_____

_____

_____

APRIL 8

OCTOBER 8

Winning has always meant much to me, but winning friends has meant the most.

~ Babe Didrikson Zaharias

Who are your closest friends?

_____

_____

_____

_____

_____

_____

Tell them today that you value their friendship.

SIX MONTHS REVIEW:

_____

_____

_____

QUOTATION SOURCE INFORMATION:

_____

_____

_____

April 9

October 9

I've missed more than 9000 shots in my career. I've lost almost 300 games. Twenty-six times I've been trusted to take the game-winning shot and missed. I've failed over and over and over again in my life, and that is why I succeed.

~ Michael Jordan

List three mistakes you've made and the lessons you've learned from them.

1. _____

_____

2. _____

_____

3. _____

_____

SIX MONTHS REVIEW:

_____

_____

_____

QUOTATION SOURCE INFORMATION:

_____

_____

_____

April 10

October 10

If I can impose my will on you, I win.

~ Peter Biadasz

Not only is there a difference between being the best and thinking you are the best, but in convincing your opponent you are better than he is, regardless of who is really more talented. How can you convince your competition you are not only better but impose your plan on them to make you victorious?

1. _____
   _____

2. _____
   _____

3. _____
   _____

Six Months Review:

_____
_____
_____

Quotation Source Information:

_____
_____
_____

APRIL 11

OCTOBER 11

I can tell you one thing. I've done this my way. I don't have anybody to blame for this win but me, and I love it.

~ John Daly

Taking responsibility in a loss is just as important as raking in the praises in a win. How do you take responsibility for your shortcomings?

1. _____

_____

2. _____

_____

3. _____

_____

SIX MONTHS REVIEW:

_____

_____

_____

QUOTATION SOURCE INFORMATION:

_____

_____

_____

APRIL 12

OCTOBER 12

For me, winning isn't something that happens suddenly on the field when the whistle blows and the crowds roar. Winning is something that builds physically and mentally every day that you train and every night that you dream.

~ Emmitt Smith

What are your dreams? List your three biggest dreams.

1. _____
2. _____
3. _____

How can each dream be fulfilled?

1. _____
2. _____
   _____
3. _____
   _____

SIX MONTHS REVIEW:

_____
_____
_____

QUOTATION SOURCE INFORMATION:

_____
_____
_____

April 13

October 13

You can't let one bad moment spoil a bunch of good ones.

~ Dale Earnhardt, Sr.

Perfectionists, no matter how successful they are, never enjoy the fruits of their hard work because they concentrate on the negative. Describe how you look at your accomplishments and put your shortcomings in a constructive perspective.

_____

_____

_____

_____

_____

_____

SIX MONTHS REVIEW:

_____

_____

_____

QUOTATION SOURCE INFORMATION:

_____

_____

_____

APRIL 14

OCTOBER 14

If you make every game a life-and-death thing, you're going to have problems. You'll be dead a lot.

~ Dean Smith

Games are supposed to be fun and teach us the lessons for a productive and constructive life. What are the most important things you have learned as the result of playing games?

1. _____

_____

2. _____

_____

3. _____

_____

SIX MONTHS REVIEW:

_____

_____

_____

QUOTATION SOURCE INFORMATION:

_____

_____

_____

APRIL 15

OCTOBER 15

He simply postures, pontificates, and postulates, but doesn't participate.

~ Richard Possett

Sometimes we just need to rest, relax, refresh, and recreate. Oftentimes, this is done in front of the tube, whether a CRT or TV. What do you do outdoors for a more active and healthy lifestyle?

1. _____

_____

2. _____

_____

3. _____

_____

SIX MONTHS REVIEW:

_____

_____

_____

QUOTATION SOURCE INFORMATION:

_____

_____

_____

APRIL 16

OCTOBER 16

Every kid around the world who plays soccer wants to be Pelé. I have a great responsibility to show them not just how to be like a soccer player, but how to be like a man.

~ Pelé

Note a few ways that you can help others learn.

1. _____
   _____

2. _____
   _____

3. _____
   _____

SIX MONTHS REVIEW:

_____
_____
_____

QUOTATION SOURCE INFORMATION:

_____
_____
_____

APRIL 17

OCTOBER 17

Most important thought, if you love someone, tell him or her, for you never know what tomorrow may have in store.

~ Walter Payton

List those whom you consider to be closest to you.

_____

_____

_____

_____

_____

_____

_____

Before you go to sleep tonight contact them to let them know the importance they have in your life.

SIX MONTHS REVIEW:

_____

_____

_____

QUOTATION SOURCE INFORMATION:

_____

_____

_____

April 18

October 18

Football is like life, it requires perseverance, self-denial, hard work, sacrifice, dedication and respect for authority.

~ Vince Lombardi

List three qualities of your "sport" you feel are much like life.

1. _____
2. _____
3. _____

Explain the importance of each.

1. _____
_____
2. _____
_____
3. _____
_____

Six Months Review:

_____
_____
_____

Quotation Source Information:

_____
_____
_____

April 19

October 19

If you watch a game, it's fun. If you play at it, it's recreation. If you work at it, it's golf.

~ Bob Hope

Make a humorous comment about your "sport."

_____

_____

_____

How can you inject humor into your life on a more regular basis?

_____

_____

_____

_____

_____

SIX MONTHS REVIEW:

_____

_____

_____

QUOTATION SOURCE INFORMATION:

_____

_____

_____

April 20

October 20

Many men go fishing all their lives without knowing that it is not fish they are after.

~ Henry David Thoreau

Maintaining focus on the right goal is sometimes difficult. How can you ensure your priorities are focused correctly?

_____

_____

_____

_____

_____

Six Months Review:

_____

_____

Quotation Source Information:

_____

_____

_____

April 21

October 21

If you cannot win, make the one ahead of you break the record.

~ Jan McKeithen

Who has inspired you to go beyond what you thought you were capable? How did they inspire you?

_____

_____

_____

How can you share these inspirations with others to assist them in getting to the next level?

_____

_____

_____

SIX MONTHS REVIEW:

_____

_____

_____

QUOTATION SOURCE INFORMATION:

_____

_____

_____

APRIL 22

OCTOBER 22

Confidence doesn't come out of nowhere. It's a result of something … hours and days and weeks and years of constant work and dedication.

~ Roger Staubach

In your opinion, is confidence a given or is it a learned trait?

_____

_____

_____

What can you do to increase your confidence?

_____

_____

_____

SIX MONTHS REVIEW:

_____

_____

_____

QUOTATION SOURCE INFORMATION:

_____

_____

_____

APRIL 23

OCTOBER 23

One man can be a crucial ingredient on a team, but one man cannot make a team.

~ Kareem Abdul-Jabbar

Is there such a thing as a team of one? _____ List the benefits of team work?

1. _____

_____

2. _____

_____

3. _____

_____

How can you become a better team player?

_____

_____

_____

SIX MONTHS REVIEW:

_____

_____

_____

QUOTATION SOURCE INFORMATION:

_____

_____

_____

April 24

October 24

The greatest teacher is observation.

~ Jeffrey Brucculeri

We learn by watching others. List successful people you will ask today to mentor you to greater success.

1. _____
2. _____
3. _____

SIX MONTHS REVIEW:

_____
_____
_____

QUOTATION SOURCE INFORMATION:

_____
_____
_____

APRIL 25

OCTOBER 25

Sports—is human life in microcosm.

~ Howard Cosell

Write down your three favorite quotations and what they mean to you.

1. _____

_____

_____

2. _____

_____

_____

3. _____

_____

_____

SIX MONTHS REVIEW:

_____

_____

_____

QUOTATION SOURCE INFORMATION:

_____

_____

_____

APRIL 26

OCTOBER 26

Be strong in body, clean in mind, lofty in ideals.

~ Dr. James Naismith

What does this quotation mean to you in each area addressed?

1. Strong in body—

_____

2. Clean in mind—

_____

3. Lofty in ideals—

_____

How can you better achieve each goal described above?

1. _____
2. _____
3. _____

SIX MONTHS REVIEW:

_____

_____

_____

QUOTATION SOURCE INFORMATION:

_____

_____

_____

April 27

October 27

The best teams have chemistry. They communicate with each other and they sacrifice personal glory for the common goal.

~ Dave DeBusschere

Teamwork is about common goals, not individual glory. In your opinion, which are the greatest teams in the history of sports?

1. _____

2. _____

3. _____

What attributes helped each team achieve greatness?

_____

_____

_____

_____

_____

Six Months Review:

_____

_____

_____

Quotation Source Information:

_____

_____

_____

April 28

October 28

The fewer rules a coach has, the fewer rules there are for the players to break.

~ John Madden

Rules can be both a help and a hindrance. Often a rule that appears to hinder is found to be a great help when the rule is understood. What are some rules that do not make sense to you?

1. _____
2. _____
3. _____

Investigate the reason for the rule and note the reason above.

If you could make one (reasonable) rule, what would it be and how would it be enforced?

_____

_____

_____

Six Months Review:

_____

_____

_____

Quotation Source Information:

_____

_____

_____

April 29

October 29

Andre Dawson has a bruised knee and is listed as day-to-day. Aren't we all?

~ Vin Scully

Being at our best every day can sometimes be a challenge. What do you do to guarantee you are at your best every day of every year?

1. _____

   _____

2. _____

   _____

3. _____

   _____

SIX MONTHS REVIEW:

_____

_____

_____

QUOTATION SOURCE INFORMATION:

_____

_____

_____

APRIL 30

OCTOBER 30

I wanted to have a career in sports when I was young, but I had to give it up. I'm only six feet tall, so I couldn't play basketball. I'm only 190 pounds, so I couldn't play football. And I have 20-20 vision, so I couldn't be a referee.

~ Jay Leno

When you were ten years old, what did you want to become?

_____

_____

_____

Did you become any of those things? _____ Why or why not?

_____

_____

_____

SIX MONTHS REVIEW:

_____

_____

_____

QUOTATION SOURCE INFORMATION:

_____

_____

_____

MAY 1

OCTOBER 31

I know we're meant to be these hard-headed, money-obsessed professionals, but we're still little boys at heart. Just ask our wives.

~ Rob Lee

Do you enjoy what you do? Why or why not?

_____

_____

_____

What makes you feel like a kid again?

_____

_____

_____

SIX MONTHS REVIEW:

_____

_____

_____

QUOTATION SOURCE INFORMATION:

_____

_____

_____

MAY 2
NOVEMBER 1

I figure practice puts your brains in your muscles.

~ Sam Snead

What three things can you do to demonstrate the value of lifelong learning?

1. _____

_____

_____

2. _____

_____

_____

3. _____

_____

_____

Next to each quality, write an action plan to develop each quality in you.

SIX MONTHS REVIEW:

_____

_____

_____

QUOTATION SOURCE INFORMATION:

_____

_____

_____

May 3
November 2

When I joined the Tour, I studied the best players to see what they did that I didn't do. I came to the conclusion that the successful players had the Three Cs: Confidence, Composure, and Concentration.

~ Bob Toski

How do the Three Cs apply to you?

Confidence—

_____

_____

Composure—

_____

_____

Concentration—

_____

_____

How can you improve in each area?

_____

_____

SIX MONTHS REVIEW:

_____

_____

_____

QUOTATION SOURCE INFORMATION:

_____

_____

_____

MAY 4

NOVEMBER 3

The worst thing about new books is that they keep us from reading the old ones.

~ John Wooden

What are some "classics" that you've never read? Make a plan to read them.

1. _____

2. _____

3. _____

SIX MONTHS REVIEW:

_____

_____

_____

QUOTATION SOURCE INFORMATION:

_____

_____

_____

May 5

November 4

You are only as good as your last win.

~ Peter Biadasz

We all have short memories. What frame of reference do you have to always consider yourself to be good in your eyes, regardless of circumstances?

1. _____

   _____

2. _____

   _____

3. _____

   _____

How can you improve on each item listed?

_____

_____

_____

SIX MONTHS REVIEW:

_____

_____

_____

QUOTATION SOURCE INFORMATION:

_____

_____

_____

MAY 6

NOVEMBER 5

If what you did yesterday seems big, you haven't done anything today.

~ Lou Holtz

You can't build a future by looking at yesterday. How can you ensure you are performing at your best today?

1. _____

_____

2. _____

_____

3. _____

_____

SIX MONTHS REVIEW:

_____

_____

_____

QUOTATION SOURCE INFORMATION:

_____

_____

_____

May 7
November 6

I watched the Indy 500 and I was thinking that if they left earlier they wouldn't have to go so fast.

~ Steven Wright

List problem-solving skills you possess.

1. _____

_____

2. _____

_____

3. _____

_____

SIX MONTHS REVIEW:

_____

_____

_____

QUOTATION SOURCE INFORMATION:

_____

_____

_____

May 8
November 7

Talent is God given. Be humble. Fame is man-given. Be grateful.
Conceit is self-given. Be careful.

~ John Wooden

Talent or *fame* or *conceit*. How can you be sure you have a healthy perspective on each in your life?

Talent—

_____

_____

Fame—

_____

_____

Conceit—

_____

_____

Six Months Review:

_____

_____

Quotation Source Information:

_____

_____

_____

May 9

November 8

If winning isn't everything, why do they keep score?

~ Vince Lombardi

This is a statement about priorities. If winning isn't everything, what do you think is?

_____

_____

_____

_____

_____

_____

Six Months Review:

_____

_____

_____

Quotation Source Information:

_____

_____

_____

May 10

November 9

An athlete cannot run with money in his pockets. He must run with hope in his heart and dreams in his head.

~ Emil Zatopek

When you are competing, either in athletics or in life, what are your primary motivators for success?

1. _____
   _____
2. _____
   _____
3. _____
   _____

How does this relate to your greatest hopes and loftiest dreams?

_____
_____
_____

SIX MONTHS REVIEW:

_____
_____
_____

QUOTATION SOURCE INFORMATION:

_____
_____
_____

May 11

November 10

Losing streaks are funny. If you lose in the beginning, you get off to a bad start. If you lose in the middle of the season, you're in a slump. If you lose at the end, you're choking.

~ Gene Mauch

Losing is never fun. When you find yourself experiencing a string of losses, how do you get on the winning track again?

1. _____

_____

2. _____

_____

3. _____

_____

How do those you admire end their losing ways?

_____

_____

_____

SIX MONTHS REVIEW:

_____

_____

_____

QUOTATION SOURCE INFORMATION:

_____

_____

_____

MAY 12
NOVEMBER 11

Finish last in your league and they call you idiot. Finish last in medical school and they call you doctor.

~ Abe Lemons

List the basic elements of your occupation.

1. _____
   _____

2. _____
   _____

3. _____
   _____

4. _____
   _____

What can you do in each element to take your performance to the next best level?

_____
_____
_____

SIX MONTHS REVIEW:

_____
_____
_____

QUOTATION SOURCE INFORMATION:

_____
_____
_____

MAY 13

NOVEMBER 12

If you want to be great at whatever you do, you have to be
committed to that certain thing. The sooner you commit, the
sooner you will achieve that goal.

~ Jeffrey Brucculeri

What are you committed to doing or becoming?

1. _____

   _____

2. _____

   _____

3. _____

   _____

Start now!

SIX MONTHS REVIEW:

_____

_____

_____

QUOTATION SOURCE INFORMATION:

_____

_____

_____

MAY 14

NOVEMBER 13

Take your victories, whatever they may be, cherish them, use them, but don't settle for them.

~ Mia Hamm

Write down your greatest victories. How can each be cherished and result in greater future victories?

1. _____

_____

2. _____

_____

3. _____

_____

SIX MONTHS REVIEW:

_____

_____

_____

QUOTATION SOURCE INFORMATION:

_____

_____

_____

MAY 15

NOVEMBER 14

Sports are preeminent in life, but need to be put in the proper perspective. Intellectual activity, a lively civic life, and good fellowship are also paramount.

~ Richard Possett

As a sports fan or athlete, what do you do outside of your sporting life to enhance the intellect, your community, and the fellowship of man? Note your activities below.

_____

_____

_____

_____

_____

_____

SIX MONTHS REVIEW:

_____

_____

_____

QUOTATION SOURCE INFORMATION:

_____

_____

_____

May 16
November 15

We can't win at home and we can't win on the road. My problem as general manager is I can't think of another place to play.

~ Pat Williams

Proper preparation will guarantee you will perform at your best, no matter the geographical location. In what ways can you move your preparation for any endeavor to the next level of "perfection"?

1. _____
   _____
2. _____
   _____
3. _____
   _____

Six Months Review:

_____
_____
_____

Quotation Source Information:

_____
_____
_____

MAY 17

NOVEMBER 16

I'll let the racket do the talking.

~ John McEnroe

There are two ways to talk—with your mouth and with your performance. In what ways can you gain a positive reputation of talking without saying a word?

1. _____

   _____

2. _____

   _____

3. _____

   _____

SIX MONTHS REVIEW:

_____

_____

_____

QUOTATION SOURCE INFORMATION:

_____

_____

_____

May 18
November 17

The most rewarding things you do in life are often the ones that look like they cannot be done.

~ Arnold Palmer

List some of your most rewarding accomplishments and the obstacles you overcame in the process of these achievements.

1. _____

_____

2. _____

_____

3. _____

_____

Six Months Review:

_____

_____

_____

Quotation Source Information:

_____

_____

_____

May 19

November 18

Golf is a good walk spoiled.

~ Mark Twain

List three sports or activities you enjoy. Define each in the Mark Twain style of humor.

1. _____

   _____

2. _____

   _____

3. _____

   _____

Enjoy the new perspective when facing challenges in each endeavor.

SIX MONTHS REVIEW:

_____

_____

_____

QUOTATION SOURCE INFORMATION:

_____

_____

_____

MAY 20

NOVEMBER 19

It is all very well to say that a man should play for the pure love of the game. Perhaps he ought, but to the working man it is impossible.

~ J. J. Bentley

How can you infuse your greatest passions into all that you desire to be successful in?

1. _____

2. _____

3. _____

SIX MONTHS REVIEW:

_____

_____

_____

QUOTATION SOURCE INFORMATION:

_____

_____

_____

MAY 21

NOVEMBER 20

Most people are in a factory from nine till five. Their job may be to turn out 263 little circles. At the end of the week they're three short and somebody has a go at them. On Saturday afternoons they deserve something to go and shout about.

~ Rodney Marsh

How do you blow off steam after a long week?

_____

_____

_____

_____

_____

_____

_____

SIX MONTHS REVIEW:

_____

_____

_____

QUOTATION SOURCE INFORMATION:

_____

_____

_____

May 22

November 21

You miss 100% of the shots you don't take.

~ Wayne Gretzky

When you attempt anything in life there may be two outcomes—you succeed or you don't succeed. How do you determine whether an attempt is worth the risk?

1. _____

2. _____

3. _____

How can you increase the number of "shots" you attempt in life?

_____

_____

_____

Six Months Review:

_____

_____

_____

Quotation Source Information:

_____

_____

_____

May 23

November 22

It's hard to beat a person who never gives up.

~ Babe Ruth

When you think of a person who does not know how to quit, of whom do you think?

_____

List three characteristics of this person as they relate to persistence?

1. _____
2. _____
3. _____

How can you incorporate these qualities into your performance?

_____

_____

_____

SIX MONTHS REVIEW:

_____

_____

_____

QUOTATION SOURCE INFORMATION:

_____

_____

_____

May 24
November 23

The ultimate victory in competition is derived from the inner satisfaction of knowing that you have done your best and that you have gotten the most out of what you had to give.

~ Howard Cosell

Before an event, how can you be thoroughly confident you have done everything you can do to prepare to face the upcoming challenges?

_____

_____

_____

After an event, how do you know you gave it your all, based on your talent, ability, and preparation?

_____

_____

_____

SIX MONTHS REVIEW:

_____

_____

_____

QUOTATION SOURCE INFORMATION:

_____

_____

_____

May 25

November 24

A winner is someone who recognizes his God-given talents, works his tail off to develop them into skills, and uses these skills to accomplish his goals.

~ Larry Bird

Many times we start working before we realize what talents we possess. Name three of your God-given talents and the key ingredients in developing these talents.

1. _____

_____

2. _____

_____

3. _____

_____

SIX MONTHS REVIEW:

_____

_____

_____

QUOTATION SOURCE INFORMATION:

_____

_____

_____

May 26

November 25

I became an optimist when I discovered that I wasn't going to win any more games by being anything else.

~ Earl Weaver

Do you consider yourself an optimist or a pessimist? _____ How does this help or hinder your performance?

1. _____
   _____

2. _____
   _____

3. _____
   _____

SIX MONTHS REVIEW:

_____
_____
_____

QUOTATION SOURCE INFORMATION:

_____
_____
_____

MAY 27

NOVEMBER 26

Never underestimate the power of dreams and the influence of the human spirit. We are all the same in this notion: The potential for greatness lives within each of us.

~ Wilma Rudolph

We all have dreams. How do you turn your dreams into reality?

1. _____

_____

2. _____

_____

3. _____

_____

How do your dreams maximize your potential?

_____

_____

_____

SIX MONTHS REVIEW:

_____

_____

_____

QUOTATION SOURCE INFORMATION:

_____

_____

_____

MAY 28

NOVEMBER 27

If you have a positive attitude and constantly strive to give your best effort, eventually you will overcome your immediate problems and find you are ready for greater challenges.

~ Pat Riley

Sometimes we focus on the problems rather than the positive results for which we are working. How can you guarantee you are constantly striving to give your best effort?

1. _____

2. _____

3. _____

SIX MONTHS REVIEW:

_____

_____

_____

QUOTATION SOURCE INFORMATION:

_____

_____

_____

May 29

November 28

You have to learn the rules of the game. And then you have to play better than anyone else.

~ Albert Einstein

What did Albert Einstein mean by this?

_____

_____

_____

_____

_____

_____

How does this quotation apply to your life?

_____

_____

_____

Six Months Review:

_____

_____

_____

Quotation Source Information:

_____

_____

_____

May 30
November 29

You can become a winner only if you are willing to walk over the edge.

~ Damon Runyon

The question is … "How badly do you want it?" The things you want in your life—are they merely wishes or committed goals? List three of your objectives in life. Think about them to determine if they are wishes or goals.

1. _____

2. _____

3. _____

Six Months Review:

_____

_____

Quotation Source Information:

_____

_____

MAY 31

NOVEMBER 30

It took me seventeen years to get 3,000 hits in baseball. I did it in one afternoon on the golf course.

~ Henry Aaron

This quotation can apply to so many sports. Record below how your "sport" can humorously relate to other endeavors. Enjoy this new perspective when things are not going as positively as you would like.

_____

_____

_____

_____

_____

_____

SIX MONTHS REVIEW:

_____

_____

_____

QUOTATION SOURCE INFORMATION:

_____

_____

_____

June 1

December 1

I will always be someone who wants to do better than others. I love competition.

~ Jean-Claude Killy

What activities are you good at and enjoy competing in? What gets your competitive juices pumping and how does it make you feel?

_____

_____

_____

_____

_____

_____

Six Months Review:

_____

_____

_____

Quotation Source Information:

_____

_____

_____

JUNE 2

DECEMBER 2

Besides pride, loyalty, discipline, heart and mind; confidence is the key to all the locks.

~ Joe Paterno

Describe your level of confidence and how you can increase it.

_____

_____

_____

_____

_____

_____

SIX MONTHS REVIEW:

_____

_____

_____

QUOTATION SOURCE INFORMATION:

_____

_____

_____

JUNE 3

DECEMBER 3

Even if you are on the right track, you'll get run over if you just sit there.

~ Will Rogers

How can you ensure you are progressing daily in your career?

_____

_____

_____

What do others in your profession do to ensure they are growing daily?

_____

_____

_____

SIX MONTHS REVIEW:

_____

_____

_____

QUOTATION SOURCE INFORMATION:

_____

_____

_____

June 4

December 4

Winning graciously is more difficult than losing graciously.

~ Peter Biadasz

Winning occurs on the field of play; life occurs off of it. How can you experience success in a way that builds others up, not to the detriment of your beaten competition?

1. _____

   _____

2. _____

   _____

3. _____

   _____

Remember, one day you may be the one beaten.

Six Months Review:

_____

_____

_____

Quotation Source Information:

_____

_____

_____

June 5

December 5

Today, I consider myself the luckiest man on the face of the Earth.

~ Lou Gehrig

Lou Gehrig stated this at a time when he knew he was dying. In what ways do you consider yourself the luckiest person on the face of the earth?

1. _____

   _____

2. _____

   _____

3. _____

   _____

SIX MONTHS REVIEW:

_____

_____

_____

QUOTATION SOURCE INFORMATION:

_____

_____

_____

JUNE 6

DECEMBER 6

The difference between old ballplayers and the new ballplayers is the jersey. The old ballplayers cared about the name on the front. The new ballplayer cares about the name on the back.

~ Steve Garvey

We are all a part of a team—whether in sports, at work, or in our family. How can we guarantee loyalty to our various teams regardless of circumstances?

1. _____

_____

2. _____

_____

3. _____

_____

SIX MONTHS REVIEW:

_____

_____

_____

QUOTATION SOURCE INFORMATION:

_____

_____

_____

June 7

December 7

Show me someone who has done something worthwhile, and I'll show you someone who has overcome adversity.

~ Lou Holtz

List three things (adversities) that you've overcome in your life and how you have become a better person because of these things.

1. _____
   _____

2. _____
   _____

3. _____
   _____

SIX MONTHS REVIEW:

_____
_____
_____

QUOTATION SOURCE INFORMATION:

_____
_____
_____

June 8

December 8

Timing is everything. It's done when it's done. Only then can you call it quits!

~ Richard Possett

To be wise at work, home, or play, you need to know when to disengage the activity, for this is what makes you successful. Note below an experience that occurred when you didn't know when to quit.

_____

_____

_____

_____

_____

_____

Six Months Review:

_____

_____

_____

Quotation Source Information:

_____

_____

_____

JUNE 9

DECEMBER 9

In order to excel, you must be completely dedicated to your chosen sport. You must also be prepared to work hard and be willing to accept constructive criticism. Without 100% dedication, you won't be able to do this.

~ Wilson Mizner

Who is your role model for dedication? What qualities does he possess?

_____
_____
_____
_____
_____
_____

SIX MONTHS REVIEW:

_____
_____
_____

QUOTATION SOURCE INFORMATION:

_____
_____
_____

June 10

December 10

People think common sense is common—but it's not.

~ Don Cherry

Humor is such an important part of a fulfilling life. What are some of the funniest moments you have experienced?

_____

_____

_____

_____

_____

_____

Remember these moments when life seems tough.

SIX MONTHS REVIEW:

_____

_____

_____

QUOTATION SOURCE INFORMATION:

_____

_____

_____

June 11

December 11

Nothing good comes in life or athletics unless a lot of hard work has preceded the effort. Only temporary success is achieved by taking short cuts.

~ Roger Staubach

Define *long term success*

How do you ensure your long term success in your most important endeavors?

SIX MONTHS REVIEW:

QUOTATION SOURCE INFORMATION:

June 12

December 12

I want to be remembered as a ballplayer who gave all I had to give.

~ Roberto Clemente

How can you be sure you are giving to your chosen profession all you have to give?

_____

_____

_____

Ask those trusted few closest to you to critique your dedication. Record the results here.

_____

_____

_____

_____

_____

SIX MONTHS REVIEW:

_____

_____

QUOTATION SOURCE INFORMATION:

_____

_____

_____

June 13

December 13

Some people are born on third base and go through life thinking they hit a triple.

~ Barry Switzer

There are many things in life we all take for granted. How can you show appreciation for the many blessings in your life?

1. _____

_____

2. _____

_____

3. _____

_____

SIX MONTHS REVIEW:

_____

_____

_____

QUOTATION SOURCE INFORMATION:

_____

_____

_____

JUNE 14

DECEMBER 14

The truth is that many people set rules to keep from making decisions.

~ Mike Krzyzewski

Sometimes the way people make a decision is by deciding not to make a decision. In what areas of your life do you have challenges in making decisions? Address and resolve this issue today.

1. _____
   _____

2. _____
   _____

3. _____
   _____

SIX MONTHS REVIEW:

_____
_____
_____

QUOTATION SOURCE INFORMATION:

_____
_____
_____

JUNE 15

DECEMBER 15

Once you are labeled 'the best' you want to stay up there, and you can't do it by loafing around. If I don't keep changing, I'm history.

~ Larry Bird

Describe the top three characteristics that you feel demonstrate your ability to change and adapt.

1. _____

_____

2. _____

_____

3. _____

_____

SIX MONTHS REVIEW:

_____

_____

_____

QUOTATION SOURCE INFORMATION:

_____

_____

_____

JUNE 16

DECEMBER 16

No one wants to quit when he's losing and no one wants to quit when he's winning.

~ Richard Petty

If you could change one thing about your career, what would it be?

_____

_____

_____

Devise an action plan to implement that change.

_____

_____

_____

_____

SIX MONTHS REVIEW:

_____

_____

_____

QUOTATION SOURCE INFORMATION:

_____

_____

_____

June 17

December 17

Baseball is not a game played on paper. On paper, they win.

~ Larry Walker

How can you help others see that although the odds are stacked against them, they can still win?

1. _____

   _____

2. _____

   _____

3. _____

   _____

Six Months Review:

_____

_____

_____

Quotation Source Information:

_____

_____

_____

JUNE 18

DECEMBER 18

Do you believe in miracles?

~ Al Michaels

What miracles have happened in your life?

1. _____

_____

2. _____

_____

3. _____

_____

4. _____

_____

SIX MONTHS REVIEW:

_____

_____

_____

QUOTATION SOURCE INFORMATION:

_____

_____

_____

JUNE 19

DECEMBER 19

That's my gift. I let that negativity roll off me like water off a duck's back. If it's not positive, I didn't hear it. If you can overcome that, fights are easy.

~ George Foreman

How do you ignore the negative and remain positive?

_____

_____

_____

_____

_____

_____

SIX MONTHS REVIEW:

_____

_____

_____

QUOTATION SOURCE INFORMATION:

_____

_____

_____

June 20

December 20

Friendships born on the field of athletic strife are the real gold of competition. Awards become corroded, friends gather no dust.

~ Jesse Owens

The greatest reward you can ever obtain is a solid relationship. What do you admire about each of your closest friends?

1. _____

_____

2. _____

_____

3. _____

_____

Today, let each person listed know how important he is to you.

SIX MONTHS REVIEW:

_____

_____

_____

QUOTATION SOURCE INFORMATION:

_____

_____

_____

JUNE 21

DECEMBER 21

Don't measure yourself by what you have accomplished, but what you should have accomplished with your ability.

~ John Wooden

Everyone has different abilities and levels of talent. What do you consider your strong points?

1. _____

2. _____

3. _____

How can each point be developed to its fullest potential?

_____

_____

_____

SIX MONTHS REVIEW:

_____

_____

_____

QUOTATION SOURCE INFORMATION:

_____

_____

_____

JUNE 22

DECEMBER 22

I am a member of a team, and I rely on the team, I defer to it and sacrifice for it, because the team, not the individual, is the ultimate champion.

~ Mia Hamm

How can you help others today?

1. _____

2. _____

3. _____

4. _____

Record the effects of each helping act.

SIX MONTHS REVIEW:

_____

_____

_____

QUOTATION SOURCE INFORMATION:

_____

_____

_____

JUNE 23

DECEMBER 23

Procrastination is one of the most common and deadliest of diseases and its toll on success and happiness is heavy.

~ Wayne Gretzky

Make a list of tasks you've been putting off, decide to get them accomplished this week, and list how you are going to complete each task.

1. _____

_____

2. _____

_____

3. _____

_____

4. _____

_____

SIX MONTHS REVIEW:

_____

_____

_____

QUOTATION SOURCE INFORMATION:

_____

_____

_____

JUNE 24

DECEMBER 24

Great champions have an enormous sense of pride. The people who excel are those who are driven to show the world and prove to themselves just how good they are.

~ Nancy Lopez

What activities can you do during the evenings and weekends to ensure you are keeping the oil that fuels your flame at a full level?

1. _____

_____

2. _____

_____

3. _____

_____

SIX MONTHS REVIEW:

_____

_____

_____

QUOTATION SOURCE INFORMATION:

_____

_____

_____

June 25

December 25

Look for your choices, pick the best one, then go with it.

~ Pat Riley

What decision are you faced with right now? What are your choices?

_____

_____

_____

_____

_____

Pick the best one and go with it!

SIX MONTHS REVIEW:

_____

_____

QUOTATION SOURCE INFORMATION:

_____

_____

June 26

December 26

I don't run away from a challenge because I am afraid. Instead, I run toward it because the only way to escape fear is to trample it beneath your feet.

~ Nadia Comaneci

List the three biggest challenges in your life. In what ways can you face each challenge to a positive end?

1. _____

_____

2. _____

_____

3. _____

_____

Six Months Review:

_____

_____

_____

Quotation Source Information:

_____

_____

_____

June 27

December 27

I don't want to be remembered for my tennis accomplishments.

~ Arthur Ashe

Frequently we want to be remembered for what we did rather than who we are.
How do you want to be remembered by those you care about the most?

1. _____

_____

2. _____

_____

3. _____

_____

List anything you need to change in your life to be remembered as you want to
be remembered.

_____

_____

_____

SIX MONTHS REVIEW:

_____

_____

_____

QUOTATION SOURCE INFORMATION:

_____

_____

_____

June 28

December 28

The winner ain't the one with the fastest car, it's the one who refuses to lose.

~ Dale Earnhardt, Sr.

List ways you can inspire others to think of themselves as winners and not losers.

1. _____
2. _____
3. _____

Would you add anything to this list?

_____

_____

Would you take anything away from this list?

_____

_____

SIX MONTHS REVIEW:

_____

_____

_____

QUOTATION SOURCE INFORMATION:

_____

_____

_____

June 29

December 29

Practice, work hard, and give it everything you have.

~ Dizzy Dean

Seems like a very simple maxim. How do you know you have practiced as you should, worked as hard as you are able, and given everything you have to your performance?

Practice—

_____

_____

Work hard—

_____

_____

Give it everything you have—

_____

_____

Six Months Review:

_____

_____

Quotation Source Information:

_____

_____

JUNE 30

DECEMBER 30

Discipline is like practice. Do something over and over and eventually you'll become very good at it.

~ Jeffrey Brucculeri

What are your best daily habits?

1. _____

_____

2. _____

_____

3. _____

_____

Commit to practicing your trade on a daily basis!

SIX MONTHS REVIEW:

_____

_____

_____

QUOTATION SOURCE INFORMATION:

_____

_____

_____

July 1

December 31

God grant me the serenity to accept the people I cannot change, the courage to change the one I can, and the wisdom to know it's me.

~ Unknown

List one thing that you want to change about yourself.

_____

_____

_____

_____

_____

_____

_____

_____

Do it!

Six Months Review:

_____

_____

_____

Quotation Source Information:

An adaptation from "The Serenity Prayer" written by Reinhold Niebuhr

_____

_____

The Finale

You've already accomplished quite a bit just by reading this book and being diligent in completing the daily life lessons. The next step now is putting what you have learned into motion.

As we touched upon in the beginning, start thinking about your desires. Where do you want to go? What do you want to achieve? Then stick to it—like the old postage stamps, they took a licking and stuck to something until they got to their destination. Today, stamps are peel-and-stick, and we can be too. Peel yourself away from the junk in your life, and stick to those things that are of value.

Be dedicated to your success. Approach your path to success wholeheartedly, and don't sway from that path. Then practice your expertise and learn from others. Strive to improve all along the way. Finally, know that there is a great cause out there, and believe it or not, it's not all about you. Serve. Serve God and serve others. Those that give, get, and they always have more to give.

Enjoy the journey to your success!

~ Jeffrey Brucculeri

CREATING A CULTURE OF CHARACTER

Congratulations!

Three cheers for making the commitment to be a more powerful person. Gleaning and utilizing the knowledge in this book are important life lessons demonstrating a great ability to do, to act, and to achieve. Developing the proper level of training, commitment, and purpose to be a more dynamic individual takes much dedication. It is the same resolve that you have shown by thoroughly and thoughtfully completing and reviewing each daily assignment.

Tom Landry has said, "Setting a goal is not the main thing. It is deciding how you will go about achieving it and staying with that plan." For the last 366 days, you have gained focus and have set some goals. You should feel good and be proud of yourself. Each day when you woke-up, you knew where you wanted to go, and you went there. Don't give up on the plan you've set before you to achieve your goals. You now clearly recognize power-driven individuals, their qualities and characteristics; use their example to inspire you to further greatness.

Knute Rockne once said, "The secret of winning football games is working more as a team, less as individuals. I play not my 11 best, but my best 11." In this book you have learned the tools for becoming your best, and you've also gathered great insight into the value of teamwork.

If you are in the first half of this book, you have learned some of the features and factors that are needed to be healthier, happier, and in harmony with others and the world. If you have finished the final six months of the assignments, you have completed a yearlong journey that has sharpened your personal skills and capabilities for a better well-being. These traits will be needed further down the road as you become a more power-driven person. John Wooden is quoted as saying, "Success comes from knowing that you did your best to become the best that you are capable of becoming." This is excellent insight. Therefore, steadfastly continue your journey toward becoming the best you can possibly be. In completing this book, you have achieved a milestone in your life by making a major scholarship investment in yourself. It was a good choice—bravo—well done!

Share your newfound understandings about power and achievement with others in your life. Help them to become powerful people by showing them how to get healthier and happier through the benefits you have learned. When you guide other people into becoming more powerful, you make yourself a wiser and more influential individual. Remember, powerful people are great givers. By investing your time and resources into this volume of work, you have learned much and have a lot to share. Now, go out into the world and share what you have, and people will be forever thankful for your healthy assistance. Your help and support will make you much more powerful, and remember ... *powerful people live powerfully*. Again, congratulations on a job well done.

~ Peter Biadasz, Richard Possett, and Jeffrey Brucculeri

The Chuncated Learning System

Ben Franklin was a brilliant gentleman and a great moral exemplar. Furthermore, he possessed a myriad of supremely admirable skills and talents. One of Franklin's many gifts was the extraordinary ability to see potential and then realize it. An area in which this aptitude was truly manifested was in the development of Franklin's moral excellence. Early on in life, he had actualized his very own *chuncated* training regimen for goodness called the thirteen virtues. Franklin wrote out a list of these ideals and had them printed in a table composed of seven columns (one for each day of the week) and thirteen rows (one for each virtue). He then placed a black spot in the appropriate square each time he failed to live that day in agreement with a particular attribute. At first, Franklin concentrated on only one quality each week, hoping to keep its row clear of spots while paying no special attention to the other characteristics. Over thirteen weeks, he worked through the whole matrix. Then he repeated the process, finding that with repetition the table got less and less spotty. Franklin wrote in his autobiography that, though he fell short of perfection, "I was, by the endeavor, a better and happier man than I otherwise should have been if I had not attempted it." With this approach, Franklin *chuncated* himself to moral excellence one day at a time. For a full explanation of the virtues, please go to www.school-for-champions.com or simply search the Internet.

As you can see, *chuncated* learning has been around since at least, if not longer than, the beginning of the Republic. It is a time-tested methodology of erudition. It is a highly effective way of developing character and personality, acquiring information, and applying knowledge. We call this technique the *Chuncated Learning System,* or "*CLS.*" *CLS* is a compelling way of cultivating positive growth and change in both your personal and professional lives. For this reason, *chuncated* learning is the chosen method that is used in the

'Power~Series' books. *CLS* is a highly cogent manner for changing personality style gradually by mastering and applying facts and ideas incrementally.

A big part of *CLS* is the small. This is because the process takes a large body of work and breaks it down into little enjoyable pieces. *CLS* is effective because it teaches a big concept in small daily bite sizes of knowledge. It is a wise-way we term *"chunking."* The approach takes a huge hunk of education and breaks it down into wee nuggets for easier learning. It is very much like baby steps; that is, scholarship in tiny short strides.

In each *'Power~Series'* book, there are exercises to be completed, reviewed, and revised over a period of one year. These tasks are assigned as home school, to be done daily in a fun, fast, and easy fashion. Empirically, we have come to know that the earthborn learn best from consistent daily study and practice. This mode easily reframes and reinforces the specific subject matter. So then, over many days and weeks, new knowledge is accumulated and a new aware-ness of oneself emerges, shaping a powerfully enhanced neo-personality style.

With each simple assignment thoroughly and thoughtfully completed, the stu-dent of a *'Power~Series'* book receives a modicum of wisdom in the form of a small reward, a little flash of accomplishment. It instills a sense of self-confi-dence by achievement. This sensation is the wonderfully good feeling of a per-sonal job well done. And each shot of "feel-good" is like a hulking reward reinforcing a newly learned chunked concept. By gradually shaping, chunk-by-chunk, your thoughts and actions, *CLS* strongly influences an improvement of your personality, giving you the power of presence and poise. It hones your latent power-driven traits and talents for a new and improved powerful you.

Furthermore, *CLS* was adopted for the *'Power~Series'* books because of its simple and straightforward approach to learning. In the hurly-burly of modern society, it is often difficult, as an adult, to continue one's education and self-development. The pressures of home, work, and family responsibilities can often restrict your personal growth and capability to improve yourself. *CLS*, with its *"chunking"* process, helps to mitigate the constraints of time materially. By simply setting aside a very small part of your busy day and focusing on learning in bite sizes, you can grow more powerful with your newly applied knowledge, one day at a time.

~ Peter Biadasz and Richard Possett

Conclusion

The conclusion is the end or the closing, the last part of a chain of events. But when you really think about it, the end of this book is actually the beginning. You have just finished the training, and now the games truly begin. That is, the game of life. It is your commencement, the time when you start putting to work your newly learned knowledge about athletes and athletics. The authors believe that there is nothing better than competitive sports, proactively engaged, to build a sound mind, a healthy body, and a stellar spirit. The implication here is that total wellness achieved from an applied craft is honed through involvement and participation. Therefore, you must take your new-found artistry of athletics into the real world and put it to good use. Realizing the utility of your new athletic perspective will make all of your life work more meaningful, productive, and powerful.

According to Ben Franklin, "Games lubricate the body and the mind." Franklin's statement is sage advice. Now, you can actualize important life lessons as a powerful athlete and person because of all the effort you have exerted to train and make yourself wiser. In the first half of this book, you absorbed the quotations and educated yourself about the author or the quotation source. You worked through the exercises. Now, you are prepared to more fully appreciate and enjoy the goodness of life due to the fact that you thoughtfully and thoroughly completed each daily lesson, the quotation, and exercise.

In the second six months of the assignments, you carefully revisited, reviewed, reevaluated, and reapplied your training. You made the necessary and appropriate adjustments to the initial output. During this period of time, you practiced what you learned. All of these concluded regimens have made you better and thus, a more powerful person through application. You did it on your own. You did it in private. Now, fully infuse this power into your daily life. Take it public. Release the newfound power of knowledge and sagacity into your personal and professional activities with energy and intensity creating a culture of character and producing a personality of power.

You already know that truly powerful people have powerful training programs. You see them at sporting venues and read about them in books, magazines, and newspapers. Every day you view them on television, learn about them on the Internet, and hear them on the radio. So, if you have carefully read this book and diligently completed the assignments, then you have made the choice to be more powerful. And success in the game of life and power in your life are nurtured by the same essential elements, perseverance and preparation. Now, begin the rest of your life knowing you have the talent and skills for more accomplishment and greater success at home, work, or play because *powerful people are guided by powerful life lessons.*

~ Peter Biadasz, Richard Possett, and Jeffrey Brucculeri

About the Authors

Peter Biadasz (pronounced bee-ahd-ish) has been teaching groups and organizations for nearly two decades. As a speaker, Peter not only shares his vision for each organization he addresses but carefully leads the members to fulfill the vision in a manner that creates win/win scenarios that are in the best interest of the organization. Having presented leadership concepts and networking skills numerous times, Peter has been known to utilize his professional trumpet talent to liven up speaking engagements.

Peter is a graduate of Florida State University. His passion for and expertise in the area of people networking has aided many over the years. There are many skills required to become a master networker, and experience has shown that the people and groups working with Peter have an increase in the quality of many of these key skills. Furthermore, an excitement for the topics at hand, as never before seen, emerges as those involved transform into distinguished and mature leaders.

The father of an incredible son and precious daughter, Peter is a lifelong runner. He has enjoyed success on the tennis court, he competes in track and field meets, and he always enjoys a good round of golf. He is also the author of *MORE LEADS: The Complete Handbook for TIPS Groups, Leads Groups, and Networking Groups* and co-author of *Increase Your Sales and Lower Your Golf Score* as well as the *'Power Series,'* of which the book you are reading is a part. Please feel free to visit Peter at www.getmoreleads.net or www.bepowerful.net.

Richard Possett is a forty-five year experienced entrepreneur and seasoned executive from the international financial and insurance services industries. As a successful businessman, Richard has spent decades managing people in new endeavors and to greater heights of performance.

Richard was born and raised in Grand Rapids, Michigan. He lived and worked for five years in Los Angeles, California, before moving to Mid-America where he and his family have resided for the last twenty years.

Richard graduated from Western Michigan University with a BBA degree, earning a major in accountancy. He is a Certified Public Accountant, board director for multiple companies, executive consultant, financialist, and past SEC-registered securities representative, accredited mortgage loan originator, and licensed insurance agent.

Richard is a former international rugby player. He served in the United States Army during the Vietnam War. He has been married to his best friend for more than forty-three wonderful years. Richard and Marilyn have three outstanding adult children (Nicole, Richard II, and Michael), three beautiful young grandchildren (Braden, Rebekah, and Hailey), and a great son-in-law, Daryl. Richard's interests are reading, writing, and walking with his wife and their two golden retrievers, Jordie and Doolie.

Richard is an award-winning author. For a complete catalog of his literary works, visit www.bepossettive.com. To contact the author personally, please feel free to e-mail him at richard@bepossettive.com. He would love to hear from everyone, everywhere.

Jeffrey Brucculeri is a radio and television broadcaster with over twenty-five years experience in the media. He is also a freelance sportswriter and play-by-play broadcaster, and his broadcast assignments have included minor league baseball, hockey, and basketball, as well as various college sports. Jeff is a member of the National Sportscasters and Sportswriters Association. Jeff is also a highly sought after motivational speaker and humorist who speaks in both church and business settings. A professional trumpet player, Jeff presents concerts in churches numerous times each year.

Jeff is a native of Jamestown, New York, where he got his start in radio, and also spent eleven years working for the local minor league baseball team. Later he became the official scorer for the Tulsa Drillers for over ten years. Jeff has spent over thirty years working in one capacity or another in minor league baseball. Jeff played college and semi-pro soccer, as well as junior college basketball, and he has enjoyed a long career as a youth sports referee, umpire, and coach. Jeff also enjoys playing golf and traveling.

A graduate of Jamestown Community College and Oral Roberts University, Jeff and his wife Colleen have two children, Joshua and Alyssa. For more information about Jeff's speaking engagements or ministry visit www.tunedinto-success.com or www.jeffbministries.com. You can contact Jeff via e-mail at jeff@tunedintosuccess.com.

A Note from the Authors

Here are some recommended 'Power~Series' books you may want to consider using to accompany your daily guide to powerful life lessons as a powerful person building a culture of character and a personality of power.

- Powerful People Have a Powerful Big "i"—*Your Daily Guide to a More Meaningful Life* by Peter Biadasz and Richard Possett

- Powerful People Have Powerful CHEE—Your Daily Guide to Synthesized Fitness of the Mind, Body, and Spirit by Peter Biadasz and Richard Possett

- Powerful People Overcome Powerful Failures—*Your Daily Guide to Becoming Powerfully Successful* by Peter Biadasz, Richard Possett, and D. Scott Cooksey

- Powerful People Play Powerful Golf—*Your Daily Guide to Golfing Powerfully* by Peter Biadasz, Richard Possett, and Matt Eidson

- Powerful People Are Powerful Leaders—*Your Daily Guide to Becoming a Powerful Leader* by Peter Biadasz and Richard Possett

- Powerful People Lead Healthy Lifestyles—*Your Daily Guide to Healthy Living* by Peter Biadasz; Marilyn S. Possett, LCSW; and Dr. David Ajibade

- Powerful People Are Powerful Performers—*Your Daily Guide to Becoming a More Power Driven Person* by Peter Biadasz and Richard Possett

Please visit www.bepowerful.net or your favorite online bookstore to purchase the above-noted books.

Index of Individuals Quoted

Aaron, Henry 83, 158

Abdul-Jabbar, Kareem 120

Alderson, M. H. 27

Ali, Muhammad 49

Andretti, Michael 55

Ashe, Arthur 58, 185

Baer, Max 63

Bannister, Roger 64, 101

Barkley, Charles 12, 54

Beamon, Bob 78

Bentley, J. J. 147

Berra, Lawrence "Yogi" 57

Biadasz, Peter 20, 43, 74, 107, 132, 162, 199

Bird, Larry 16, 152, 173

Bol, Manute 80

Bradshaw, Terry 19

Brock, Lou 75

Broun, Haywood Hale 89

Brucculeri, Jeffrey 8, 41, 72, 121, 140, 188, 200

Bryant, Paul "Bear" 31

Campanella, Roy 94

Carril, Pete 95

Cervantes, Miguel 42

Cherry, Don 168

Clemente, Roberto..98, 170

Comaneci, Nadia 184

Coryell, Don 87

Cosell, Howard 122, 151

Daly, John 108

Daugherty, Duffy...21

Dean, Dizzy 187

DeBusschere, Dave 124

Dorsett, Tony 32

Earnhardt, Dale Sr. 110, 186

Edison, Thomas..37

Einstein, Albert 156

Erving, Julius 9

Finley, Charlie O..50

Ford, Henry 3

Foreman, George 177

Garvey, Steve 164

Gehrig, Lou 163

Gretzky, Wayne 149, 181

Hamm, Mia 141, 180

Holtz, Lou...13, 81, 133, 165

Hope, Bob 116

Jackson, Bo...33

Jackson, Phil 99

Jefferson, Thomas 17

Jenner, Bruce 61

Johnson, Ervin"Magic" 23

Johnson, Samuel 85

Jordan, Michael 40, 106

Killy, Jean-Claude 34, 159

King, Billie Jean 103

Kitt, A. J. 14

Knight, Ray 56

Krzyzewski, Mike 172

Lasorda, Tommy 52

Lee, Rob 128

LeMond, Greg 70

Lemons, Abe 139

Leno, Jay 127

Lombardi, Vince 47, 76, 93, 115, 136

Lopez, Nancy 182

Lott, Ronnie 35

MacArthur, Douglas 66

Madden, John 125

Malone, Moses 45

Marsh, Rodney 148

Mauch, Gene 138

McEnroe, John 144

McKeithen, Jan 118

Michaels, Al 176

Miller, Shannon 86

Mizner, Wilson 167

Naismith, James 123

Namath, Joe 15

Newcombe, Don 97

Noll, Chuck 18

Owens, Jesse 178

Paige, Satchel 62

Palmer, Arnold 36, 145

Paterno, Joe..39, 67, 84, 90, 160

Payton, Walter 114

Pelé 113

Petty, Richard..174

Plato 96

Player, Gary 92

Possett, Richard 24, 53, 77, 112, 142, 166, 199

Richards, Bob..46

Riley, Pat 29, 44, 88, 155, 183

Rogers, Will 161

Rudolph, Wilma 154

Runyon, Damon 157

Ruth, Babe 79, 150

Sayers, Gale 71

Schultz, George 68

Scott, Dave 10

Scully, Vin 126

Seneca 25

Shoemaker, Bill 26

Smith, Dean..111

Smith, Emmitt 109

Snead, Sam..129

Solomon..7

Staubach, Roger 119, 169

Strauss, Robert..38

Street, Picabo 60

Switzer, Barry...171

Taylor, Bill 91

Thoreau, Henry David 117

Tomba, Alberto 28

Toski, Bob 130

Twain, Mark 82, 146

Valvano, Jim 69

Waitley, Denis 48

Walker, Herschel 59

Walker, Larry 175

Ward, William A 30

Weaver, Earl 153

Williams, Pat 143

Wooden, John 22, 51, 73, 104, 131, 135, 179

Woods, Tiger 102

Wright, Steven 100, 134

Young, Steve...11

Zaharias, Babe Didrikson 105

Zatopek, Emil 137

Index of Topics Quoted

Ability 13, 56, 151, 179

Achievement 35

Adversity 15, 30, 38, 64, 81, 90, 165, 184

Attitude 13, 73, 86, 94, 100, 110, 115, 128, 132, 135, 153, 155, 158, 163, 171, 175, 177

Character 81, 89, 96, 104, 123

Commitment 29, 140

Competition 159

Concentration 56, 130

Confidence 19, 31, 39, 119, 130, 160

Courage 46, 82, 189

Death 21

Decisions 172, 183

Dedication 78, 167, 170

Desire 8, 57, 86, 127

Determination 52

Discipline 103, 149

Dreams 57, 109, 154

Enthusiasm 40

Fear 62, 63, 184

Focus..26, 65, 177, 133

Friendship 105, 178

Goals..10, 33, 123, 127, 157

Health 9, 20, 77, 112, 126

Helping 16

Humility...54

Humor 97, 116, 146, 158, 168

Influence 41, 53, 107, 142, 144, 162

Inspiration 32, 37, 60, 69, 118, 186

Intelligence...95

Learning 22, 34, 61, 99, 106, 111, 115, 121, 129

Legacy...44, 185

Life 21

Losing...18, 138

Love 80, 114

Loyalty 164

Mentoring...12, 102, 113, 118, 121, 180

Miracles 176

Motivation 13, 34, 34, 137

Opportunity...25, 47

Passion 147

Perseverance...69, 83, 85, 103

Persistence 150

Playing 111

Potential 51, 76

Preparation 42, 43, 74, 85, 95, 126, 143, 151

Pride..7

Priorities...75, 80, 117, 136

Problem-solving 134

Procrastination 14, 181

Professional 67

Purpose 65

Quitting 36, 38, 71, 166

Quote 122, 156

Reading 22, 131

Relaxation 148

Responsibility 108

Risk...55, 149

Rules..125, 156

Self-improvement 11, 27, 33, 37, 70, 84, 88, 106, 142, 161, 173, 174, 182, 188

Self-respect 49

Serenity 189

Success......................................24, 47, 50, 55, 72, 101, 137, 145, 147, 169

Talent 152

Teaching..102

Teamwork 16, 23, 79, 87, 91, 98, 120, 124, 180

Thinking 48, 68

Time management 93

Training 59, 70

Winning 18, 66, 109, 136, 141, 162, 175, 186

Wisdom 7, 58, 189

Work ethic....................................17, 46, 50, 59, 76, 92, 139, 168, 187

Note: Many quotations may fit into more than one category.